PRAISE FOR
DOORWAY
TO THE SOUL

"Dr. Scolastico's book helps you feel the magnificence of yourself as an eternal soul, and as a vibrant human being. It takes you on a personal journey toward your larger existence, revealing your purpose on earth, and giving you ways to fulfill that purpose."

—Louise L. Hay, bestselling author of
You Can Heal Your Life and
Life! Reflections on Your Journey

"I have never believed that we are just dropped off here on earth. *DOORWAY TO THE SOUL* reminds me of the truth of our spiritual origins. When I read this book, my heart and mind were deeply touched."

—Les McCann, jazz musician

Also by Ron Scolastico, Ph.D.

THE EARTH ADVENTURE
Your Soul's Journey Through Physical Reality

HEALING THE HEART, HEALING THE BODY
A Spiritual Perspective on Emotional, Mental, and Physical Health

REFLECTIONS
Inspired Wisdom on: Gods and Symbols; The Human Mind; Angels and Guides; Education; Healing Addictions; and Healing the Hurt Child

Ron Scolastico, Ph.D.

Doorway
to the
Soul

How to Have a Profound Spiritual Experience

POCKET BOOKS

New York   London   Toronto   Sydney   Tokyo   Singapore

POCKET BOOKS, a division of Simon & Schuster Inc.
1230 Avenue of the Americas, New York, NY 10020

Copyright © 1995 by Ron Scolastico, Ph.D.

All rights reserved, including the right to reproduce
this book or portions thereof in any form whatsoever.
For information address Scribner, 1230 Avenue
of the Americas, New York, NY 10020

ISBN: 0-671-53510-2

First Pocket Books trade paperback printing April 1997

10 9 8 7 6 5 4 3 2 1

POCKET and colophon are registered trademarks of
Simon & Schuster Inc.

Cover photo © 1995 Doug Plummer / Photonica

Printed in the U.S.A.

I do not need to wait until I am removed from the things around me in the physical world to gain entry into the spirit realm. I already exist and live in the latter much more truly than in the former. Heaven does not lie beyond the grave; it is here already, pervading all of nature, and its light rises in every pure heart.

JOHANN GOTTLIEB FICHTE, 1806

For my beloved wife,
Susan Scolastico,
and for those who seek
a larger vision of life.

Contents

———— ✳ ————

Contents

Contents

CHAPTER FIVE

Your Beginning Attunement   *109*

CHAPTER SIX

A Deeper Experience of Your Soul   *123*

CHAPTER SEVEN

Your Transformation   *153*

Contents

Acknowledgments

———— ✳ ————

I want to express my deep appreciation to my agent, Harvey Klinger, and to Susan Moldow at Scribner for her insight and sensitivity in editing this book.

I am also very grateful to Don Marrs, Paige Reynolds, Anna Marie Wilzcek, and Ellen Seely for their friendship, and for their wise suggestions for the content and structure of the book.

My appreciation goes to Louise Hay and her staff at Hay House for their encouragement and support.

And, finally, a special thank-you to Barbara DeAngelis for her inspiration, and for her help in bringing this book into being.

DOORWAY

to the

SOUL

A Vast Source of Knowledge

———— ✳ ————

In my career as a Transpersonal Psychologist, I have worked with thousands of people who are hungry for a deeper experience of life. They want to know why they are here on earth; what created them; what happens to them after they die. They want to know what part they themselves play in the cosmic drama that is unfolding in the universe around them. In essence, they want to know about the *spiritual* aspects of their existence.

Many of the people with whom I work are fascinated by published accounts of dramatic spiritual experiences. They are particularly impressed by reports of *near-death* occurrences in which a person's physical body is clinically dead for a brief period, but the conscious awareness moves off into a deep spiritual experience. These reports bring insights into the spiritual world that many people find very inspiring.

I believe that such accounts are compelling because they take us where most people are not yet able to go: *beyond physical reality*. They bring us fascinating knowledge about the spiritual aspects of life that many people long for, but have not yet been able to attain on their own.

Another strong appeal of near-death reports is the hope they give us that there is more to life than the constant stream of negative events described in newspapers and magazines and on television. Many people feel the heaviness of negative world events pressing in upon them. They feel frustrated and worried about the pressures and challenges of their daily lives. Longing for a more joyful feeling about life, they are inspired by near-death reports because, in the near-death experience, ordinary people come to the threshold of a doorway between the challenging physical world and a larger, more beautiful nonphysical realm that lies beyond ordinary reality. They pass through that doorway for a brief moment and then bring back inspiring, transformative experiences of a majestic spiritual dimension where there are no limits to their personal expression. Those who have such experiences gain a deep feeling of joy in their lives, and they come to believe that there can be great goodness and purpose in life. Passing through the doorway to a larger reality also seems to enable them to more confidently master the challenges of their daily life.

In this book I will share with you what I have discovered by actually passing through a doorway to a vast spiritual reality more than 14,000 times—a feat that I have accomplished without having a near-death experience. By learning to make certain important inner adjustments, I have been able to consistently enter extremely deep states of consciousness that enable me to go beyond the physical world into the most wondrous spiritual reality imaginable. I hope that I can help you make the same inner adjustments so that you, too, can have your own profound spiritual experiences.

In the thousands of journeys that I have taken into the spiritual world, I have not only had amazing experiences of inspiration, but I have also been able to tap into a vast source of all-encompassing wisdom that lies outside ordinary human awareness. Drawing from that source, I have brought back inspiring knowledge that has not only helped me create joy and growth in my own life, but has also bene-fited thousands of people throughout the world—leading many of them to the profound experience of spiritual realities that they desire.

When I enter the expanded state of consciousness that enables me to pass through the doorway between physical reality and the spiritual realms, I believe that I am using intuitive abilities that are available to everyone. Most people simply have not taken the time to discover and open these abilities. If only they knew how marvelous the experience could be, they would be more motivated to make such an opening.

As I enter the deep state of consciousness that leads to the spiritual source of wisdom, I pass into the most amazing realm of beauty, harmony, and unlimitedness. There is nothing for my physical senses to perceive, for there is no physical matter. But there is an experience of incredible unending love and well-being. It feels as if the nurturing power of this realm permeates everything that exists. I also experience an absolute certainty that we, as human beings, are always deeply cherished by this spiritual presence. Our *being* is never in any danger because we are a part of this love energy. It is so clear that life constantly sustains and encourages us to fulfill the greatest potential that we have within ourselves. I am fully aware that our personal existence is always ongoing, that it is not diminished by physical death. There is a very deep feeling of perfection that I recognize as a quality that lives within all beings. There is also an endless flow of inspiring knowledge that can answer any possible question that might be asked about life.

I first learned to make this deep connection to spiritual realities in the 1970s, just after I completed my Ph.D. degree in Humanistic Psychology and Human Communications at a large midwestern university. At that time, even though I was pleased about my academic pursuits, I was very troubled about life. I worried a lot about the state of the world. I saw so much negativity around me—social conflict, poverty, crime, individuals being cruel and unkind to one another—that I was discouraged about the possibility of people ever healing their differences and coming together in understanding.

Yet my most troubling problem was that I had no ongoing source of *inspiration* to give me hope about life. Although I had studied psychology, philosophy, and spiritual studies for many years, and had been practicing meditation for ten years, I had never directly experienced the deep, ongoing beauty of the spiritual realm. I had only read about it in books. I had never broken through the barriers of ordinary human experience to verify the existence of spiritual realities for myself. I had gone beyond the limits of the physical world only once, and that was very frightening.

I was eight years old. It was a warm summer afternoon, and I was lying on my bed, reading a book. All of a sudden I began to feel as if I were expanding. I seemed to be growing larger than my body. I started to swell and fill up my room. I became a huge ball of awareness, and I seemed to be floating near the ceiling. In terror, I jumped up out of bed, which snapped me back into my body, and I ran out of my room.

That experience was so frightening that I immediately forced it out of my mind. So from that time to the period of my inner struggles in the seventies, I had blocked out the memory of that disturbing childhood experience. As far as I was consciously aware, I had always been limited to my ordinary perceptions of life.

During my difficult period at the university I was also struggling with a feeling of disconnectedness in my personal life. None of the wisdom that I had gained from all of my studies seemed to help with the feeling of emptiness that I had inside. I was not creating deep relationships with the people around me. Also, even though I was planning to teach at a university, I had no real enthusiasm about the prospect. Actually, I felt that I really had no purpose in my life.

At that point I met a fascinating woman named Lina who gave "psychic readings." Even though I considered an intellectual study of spiritual realities to be a valid pursuit for intelligent people, at that time, because of a certain academic snobbishness that I had developed, I felt that most psychics were, at best, ignorant and, at worst, outright charlatans who took money from the gullible. Yet, somehow, one cold winter evening I found myself trudging off through the lightly falling snow to have a reading with this intriguing woman.

On that walk I had a strange experience that set into motion a most profound transformation in my life. As I was making my way through the darkness, comfortably snuggled under the hood of my down jacket, I started wondering why I was wasting my time on a psychic reading. I stopped for a minute and considered forgetting the whole thing and going back home.

Instead, I looked around at the beauty of the still, cold night. I began to feel touched by the tranquillity of the gently falling snow as it sparkled in the streetlight. Then I glanced up and saw a full moon, brilliant and majestic against the black sky.

At that moment I was simply staring at the moon, without any particular thoughts in my mind, when I suddenly began to feel a slight tingling in my body. Then I noticed that my awareness seemed to be expanding, becoming larger. My vision was growing strangely acute, giving everything I saw a mysterious new brilliance. I began to feel extremely alert, particularly sensitive to everything around me.

What followed was a most profound feeling of exhilaration that seemed to fill my entire being. I felt very warm and intensely alive, as though everything around me was infused with this stimulating "energy" that seemed to be flowing through me.

As I stood motionless in the snow, I seemed to be caught in a most amazing moment. I felt deeply touched by the pure, unending beauty of life. I was suspended in a timeless experience, enveloped in a deeply moving energy of love, waiting with intense anticipation to see what the next moment would bring. I had an overwhelming feeling that something very important was about to happen to me.

Then a most powerful thought instantly appeared in my mind. It was so dramatically different from my own way of thinking that it seemed as if it came from somewhere beyond myself. The thought was: *"This is a night that will change your life."*

Feeling confused and a bit disoriented by this unusual experience, I quickly made my way to Lina's house. By the time I arrived, because of my habitual skepticism and mistrust of anything that I could not grasp with my intellect, I had convinced myself that the unusual experience in the moonlight was nothing more than my imagination.

Yet, in spite of my skepticism and misgivings, the reading with Lina was a deeply moving experience for me. She helped me identify the source of the nagging emptiness that I had been feeling. With her help I saw that I had closed myself emotionally because of my past pain and suffering. I had learned to hide behind my intellect in order not to feel my emotional pain.

Her reading also helped me recognize the first stirrings of a spiritual experience. It was very subtle, and I was not clear about what it was at the time, but I had an inner feeling of something warm and loving beginning to open within me.

As I had more readings with Lina, we became good friends. Then she introduced me to Cora, who did similar readings. In a matter of months, working with the wise counsel that I received from readings with these two women, I made some very deep emotional openings. Touched by the wisdom of their work, and moved by their personal sensitivity and kindness, I began to experience more love in my day-to-day life. I was even feeling more hopeful about the general state of the world.

Then, in one reading with Cora, I was shocked when I was told that I had the ability to enter a deep state of consciousness, draw upon a spiritual source of wisdom, and give guidance to others by speaking from that deep state. Indeed, her reading informed me that I had "promised" to do such work in this lifetime.

At that time I was in my late thirties, and I was convinced

that I had no such ability. So I was skeptical about what I was told. Yet since I had come to trust Cora's readings, I decided to conduct an experiment to test myself. I set up a tape recorder beside the chair where I meditated each morning. Then every day after my meditation, with my eyes closed and trying to stay in the meditative state, I would reach over, turn on the tape recorder, and begin to speak my thoughts out loud.

I would usually talk for ten minutes or so. Then I would come out of the meditative state and listen to the tape to see if anything was said that went beyond what I consciously knew. I was not surprised to find that these meditation speakings seemed to be nothing more than my own thoughts and ideas spoken in an ordinary way.

Yet even though I felt that the source of these utterances was simply me talking in a relaxed state, each time I did a period of this speaking I felt a deep sense of peace. It was very pleasant, more so than my meditation experience that preceded the speaking. So I continued to do this "thinking out loud" every day.

After a few months of this practice I began to have some unusual experiences. My voice suddenly took on a different sound, along with a strange accent. Then I began to give information about friends that seemed to help them. Still, I felt that what was being said during these speaking sessions was coming from my own mind, conscious or unconscious. Even though I was beginning to experience some deep feelings of inner opening stirring within me as I learned to make adjustments that allowed me to release more and more into the speaking process, I continued to be skeptical about my ability to tap into a spiritual source of wisdom.

For several months I made tapes of my speaking for various friends, always alone in the privacy of my room. Then one day Lina convinced me that I needed to do a "live" session for her. Although I was reluctant, and somehow embarrassed by the idea of sitting in front of another person talking in a strange voice, I finally agreed to give it a try. This turned out to be the opening that would launch me into a new career.

As I sat down at Lina's house to do my first formal "reading," I was very nervous. I procrastinated and made excuses for a while. Lina encouraged me by entering her deep state of consciousness to give me some suggestions on how to begin. With that prompting I was finally able to start the speaking for her.

At first there was a general statement about Lina's life. Then Lina asked questions and I answered. During all of this I felt the same as I did in my daily private utterances.

After my initial nervousness I became deeply relaxed and began to feel the sense of peacefulness that always came during the speakings. Yet, as far as I could tell, the words being spoken to Lina appeared to be coming from my own mind.

Then something quite unusual began to happen. A very strange sensation of *lightness* started to infuse my entire body. I began to feel as if I could just float away from my body. I seemed to be as light as air.

This was followed by a very strong feeling of being *expanded*. I seemed to be growing *larger*, going beyond what I had always felt to be *me*. Instead of my normal feeling of being *inside* my body, I was becoming an expanding, free-floating awareness that began to fill the entire room. What was so amazing to me was that I had no part in creating this experience. It was happening to me spontaneously, as if the experience was being given to me by something beyond myself.

As this feeling of expansion continued, I began to experience a most profound feeling of *love*, the depth of which astonished me. I had never before felt anything like it. It seemed as if everything in life was being permeated by this unbelievable love.

Even the skeptical part of me was overwhelmed by the astounding experience of being expanded by this love. It was absolutely clear that this was not my imagination. Something startlingly *real* was happening to me. The feeling of love was so intense that I was filled with tears of joy. I was amazed when I realized that *I had entered a realm of existence beyond ordinary reality*.

For a while I was completely caught up in this most astonishing experience. My voice had stopped speaking to Lina when the experience began, so I was drifting silently in a remarkable world of vast beauty and love. My physical body was gone. I was floating about as a vibrant, enlightened totality of awareness.

I have no idea how long this amazing state of expansion lasted. I had lost all awareness of my physical body. Then suddenly I felt a strong force of energy pushing out from within me, and my voice began to speak to Lina again.

But as my voice spoke it was very different from all of the "talking out loud" that I had done in the past. Now the words that were coming forth were not mine. They were being chosen by something beyond my own conscious awareness. They were somehow being placed into me by a source that was profoundly wise and loving. The words seemed to be spoken *through* me in a way that felt wonderful and sublime.

Since I was not deciding what was being said, I heard only one word at a time as my voice spoke. Thus, I had no idea of what was going to be said until a sentence was completed.

I listened in total fascination at what the words were telling Lina. They began by explaining to her that the reason for the long silence that had just occurred was that *I had left my physical body*. Then the voice told Lina that my consciousness had to leave my body so that I could draw upon a vast realm of truth that I was now tapping into. She was told that I was being infused with a tremendous energy of universal wisdom and love that would help me in my personal growth and in my ability to tap into this source of wisdom in the future.

Then the voice told her something that shook me to my depths. It said, "*The experience of expansion that Ron is now having was first implanted in him when he was eight years old so that it could be returned to him at this time so that he would believe.*"

The voice continued to speak to Lina, but I was so stunned by what had been said that I heard nothing else that was spoken. I was suddenly remembering that long-ago forgotten experience of my eight-year-old self, and I realized that it was the same experience that was happening to me now. All at once any sense of past and present collapsed. There was only the brilliance of the moment in which that past experience of the eight-year-old child was now merged with my incredible experience of love and expansion in the present moment. In that moment I realized that the two experiences that were now fusing into one were the only times in my life that I had ever *consciously broken through the boundaries of physical reality*. I had gone beyond the physical world into an amazing nonphysical reality of majesty, wisdom, and love, and I longed to go deeper.

After that experience with Lina, I discovered that in my meditation period each day I was loosening my consciousness in a way that was bringing me closer and closer to the doorway to the spiritual realms. I began to do face-to-face speaking sessions for other people similar to the one I had done for Lina. As I did these sessions day after day, my inner experience deepened, and I learned to make the delicate adjustments of consciousness that allowed me to enter the spiritual dimensions of reality to draw upon the vast source of knowledge and wisdom.

Not only was my personal experience growing richer and fuller from this work, but also the people for whom I did these speaking sessions seemed to be genuinely touched and benefited by what they were given. The sessions were providing them with valuable information about their personality and their life that went far beyond my own conscious knowledge.

Since these beginning experiences many years ago, I have entered the spiritual realm to provide information and guidance for thousands of individuals throughout the world. I have created numerous audiotapes of wisdom that have been helpful to many people. And this is the fourth book of inspired knowledge that I have drawn from the apparently limitless source. It has been a great joy for me to see so many people use these books and tapes to bring about beneficial and meaningful changes in their lives.

I have written this Introduction in my own words. The rest of this book has been "written" by the vast source of wisdom that I draw upon in the nonphysical world. While I am in that amazing realm, the knowledge from the source is spoken into a tape recorder. The tapes are then transcribed, and I edit the transcriptions for clarity and ease of understanding.

When I am speaking the knowledge from the source, my conscious mind is not in control, and I do not choose the words. It seems as if the source of knowledge is using my human vocabulary to communicate wisdom that I do not have in my own mind. Therefore, when you read this book you can feel that the source of knowledge is speaking directly to you, bringing you a far-reaching perspective of life that can help you see beyond the limits of human awareness.

You will notice that this book addresses some of the *psychological* aspects of our human experience, as well as the spiritual dimensions of life. That is because it is necessary for us to have an understanding of ourselves as individuals in order to make the adjustments in our attitudes and beliefs that are necessary for attaining a deep spiritual experience.

In Chapter One, "Expanding Your Vision of Yourself," the groundwork is laid for an understanding of your true nature. There are insights into your larger existence that can stimulate your thoughts and feelings in a way that will be very helpful in creating a deep spiritual experience.

Chapter Two, "Your Process of Growth," presents important ways to work inwardly in order to begin to open yourself to the deeper realities of life. Suggestions are also made for using the mind in a powerful way to stimulate the inner process of growth that will lead to an experience of spiritual realms.

The way spiritual growth is unintentionally blocked by negative feelings is explored in Chapter Three, "Transforming Negativity." Many difficult emotional experiences, such as fear, sadness, and depression, are discussed in a way that shows the cause of such feelings and reveals ways to heal them. This chapter will show you why it is so important to heal your negative thoughts and feelings before you attempt to create a deep spiritual experience.

Chapter Four, "Building a Foundation for Your Spiritual Breakthrough," shows you how to develop attitudes toward your spiritual practice that will prepare you for a deep spiritual experience. It explores the relationship between love and your spiritual opening. It throws light upon spiritual guidance and helps you be aware of guidance in a sensitive way. Many of the confused attitudes that people have about spiritual realities are cleared up. This knowledge will help you begin your spiritual opening with clarity and wisdom.

In Chapter Five, "Your Beginning Attunement," you are given a specific method for making a beginning spiritual opening. The inner process explored here can give you the practice that you need to expand your awareness in preparation for a full spiritual experience. It is the foundation for the deeper process presented in the following chapter.

Chapter Six, "A Deeper Experience of Your Soul," offers inspiring guidance for entering more deeply into the spiritual realities of life. There is a step-by-step method for opening yourself to the profound spiritual experience that you desire. Wise suggestions are given for working with your inner experience on a day-to-day basis in order to learn how to fully penetrate the limits of human perception and attain a larger vision of the spiritual world.

In the final chapter, Seven, "Your Transformation," you are given an inspiring vision of the expanded experiences that you can have in the future by opening yourself to the larger realities of life. You are shown how to choose your direction for the future so that you may express your full potential and achieve the important purposes in your life.

I believe that the knowledge presented in this book can help you learn to step through the inner doorway between the physical world and what lies beyond. You do not need to have a near-death experience in order to enter the spiritual realities of life. You have an innate ability to make an inner opening that will allow you to experience what lies beyond the physical world.

If you work with this book with patience and sensitivity, I believe that you can learn to make that opening and have your own profound spiritual experiences. As you consistently create such experiences of your spiritual nature, and bring those experiences back into your daily affairs in the physical world, you can create a richer, more meaningful life. You can experience the deep satisfaction and love that you have always desired in your life.

CHAPTER ONE

Expanding Your Vision of Yourself

———— ✳ ————

M any people become so caught up in the physical world that they forget that their present human life is temporary, that it will eventually end in death. They do not realize that they have a beautiful non-physical being that has an ongoing existence that will continue after the death of their physical body. As they lose themselves in their temporary human life, with its painful challenges and feelings of limitation and deprivation, they can come to feel small and unimportant. They can lose sight of their true goodness and magnificence.

This human confusion can be understood by imagining that you have been given a large, clear stone that sparkles. You are quite poor, and in your experience all such stones have been glass. Thus, you say, "What a pretty piece of glass," and you carry it with you as a good luck charm. Each day, in your poverty, you toil for pennies to earn your bread, carrying your piece of glass with you. One day you come to a marketplace and show your good luck piece to a jeweler. He tells you, "This is a priceless diamond. You are very wealthy."

The truth is that you were *always* wealthy, but you did not know it *because of your attitude toward your treasure*. In the same way you have always been a worthy, valuable person, aligned with your *spiritual* being that springs forth from loving non-physical realities. Yet when you limit your vision of yourself to the small human experience, you can develop an attitude toward yourself that can cause you to feel, "My human expression is not worth much." You do not know that the "glass" of your human personality is a diamond, a treasure. You do not know that your human personality is a beautiful, priceless expression of wonderful nonphysical forces.

For those who are not naturally curious about discovering the treasure of their true being, and who are not interested in looking beyond the physical reality, the first stirrings of a desire for a greater vision of life can often come about through severe challenge, or catastrophe in their physical world. For example, imagine that you are a young successful and wealthy businessperson. You have a beautiful family. You have decided that your only purpose in life is to gain pleasure for yourself, so you believe that there is no need to do anything different for the rest of your life. But imagine that your true purpose in this lifetime is not only to fulfill your own desires for personal pleasure, but also to establish deep, loving relationships with other people in order to better humanity. Such a purpose would require you to be emotionally open to others, to feel compassion for them, and to find deeper purpose and meaning in your human relationships that would take you beyond your own self-indulgence.

As such a businessperson who is blindly rushing down a path of self-involvement, you are not consciously aware of this larger purpose. You are lost in your pursuit of pleasure and your preoccupation with physical reality. Thus, you are not likely to make any change in your life.

Then imagine that your small child suddenly becomes seriously ill. The feelings of fear and suffering that you experience are so strong that none of the previously important things in your life—work, money, play—can ease your pain. You fall into such a deep despair that you begin to question the purpose of a life in which your child might be taken from you. You realize that if your child should die, you could find no way to fill the void in your life. Such a personal trauma could motivate you to look beyond your self-indulgent search for pleasure in the physical world. It could drive you to search for meaningful answers to existence that go beyond life and death.

Because of your suffering, you might begin to ask, "What good is all the money in the world if my child is taken from me? What is the purpose of rushing to succeed in life if I cannot succeed in saving my child?"

Imagine that your child recovers. Even though you are enormously relieved, the questioning brought about by your personal crisis could begin an inner search for deeper meaning in your life, for something that can sustain you when the physical world seems terribly dark and hopeless. Such a search could lead you out of the self-preoccupation that had previously trapped you. It could open you to a deeper love for the people around you. This could eventually lead you to an awareness of the true purpose for which you came into your present human life. In time, such a search could lead you to a direct experience of your true being.

Of course, you can begin your own quest for truth in a more positive, creative way. You do not need disaster to motivate you. At the present moment you might feel relatively satisfied with your physical life, but you may have a hunger to know more about the vastness of the universe in which you live. You might be motivated by a desire to understand the mystery of the endless cycles of human life and death through countless ages. You might ask, "Is all of this vastness within the universe constructed simply for me to spend my days in the pursuit of physical pleasures? Are there not larger and deeper purposes for the constant unfoldment of human life on earth, generation after generation?"

Such questioning can set you out upon your own quest to understand the deeper mysteries of life. It can lead you to expand your vision of life so that you can go beyond the present limitations of human perception.

If you could view yourself in this moment without the normal limits of human perception, you would see that you now have within yourself the key to achieving all that you desire in your human experience. That key is your *awareness*. By learning to use the power of your awareness in new and expanded ways, you can break through the limits of human perception to explore dimensions of your being that lie beyond physical reality. You can learn to draw upon those nonphysical aspects of your being in ways that will enable you to master the challenges of your life, express your full creative abilities, create the depth of love that you desire, and achieve a profound joy and fulfillment in your daily experience on earth.

To prepare the way for the expansion of your awareness, you can begin to create a new understanding of who *you* really are.

YOUR DUAL EXISTENCE

As a human being in a physical body, you are experiencing only a small portion of your true Self. Ordinarily, you are not consciously aware that while you are living in human form you have a *simultaneous* ongoing existence as a nonphysical being.

To begin to form a clear vision of your existence as a spiritual being, and to loosen any rigid ideas that you may presently have about the nonphysical realities of life, it can be helpful to start with a simple image. Imagine that you are walking in a forest and you come to a shallow stream. You wish to wade across the stream, so you take off your shoes, hold them in your hand, and step into the stream.

Then imagine that a naive native who is unfamiliar with shoes observes you in the stream with your shoes in your hand. Based upon that observation, the native decides that you are a being who always carries shoes in your hand. The native assumes that such a manifestation is the truth of your entire existence. What the native does not realize is that carrying shoes in your hand is a *temporary* expression of you that occurs only while you are crossing the stream. You have a much larger life beyond the stream during which you wear your shoes.

As you live your present human life, it is similar to crossing the stream, except that you need to imagine that there are *two* of you. The *first you* is crossing the stream with your shoes in your hand. That is your present human personality that is *temporarily* living in a physical body, temporarily existing within the limits and challenges of physical reality. The *second you* is much larger. At the same time that the first you is wading across the stream with your shoes in your hand, the second you is standing outside the stream, wearing shoes. The second you is yourself existing *permanently* as a nonphysical spiritual being who is not limited by the narrowness of physical reality.

Your earth life is only a small, temporary portion of a much larger existence that you continue to have as a nonphysical being outside the "stream" of human life. Yet because your present conscious awareness is dominated by your human experience in the physical world, and because it is difficult for the human mind to understand that you can be in two places at one time—that you can exist simultaneously as a physical human being *and* as a nonphysical spiritual being—it is usually difficult for you to become aware that you have an existence beyond the physical world.

Yet the truth is that you exist within the limits of physical reality only while a portion of your larger Self is temporarily living in a human body—only while you are crossing the stream do you carry your shoes in your hand. However, as a human being you are often the naive person watching yourself cross the stream with your shoes in your hand—you believe that the small portion of your existence that you are now living in human life is your entire being. You cannot see that beyond your temporary human expression, you are now existing in a vast realm that is not physical, that is unlimited, that has an eternal beauty and magnificence. You cannot perceive that in your true existence you are a being that, in present language, can be called a *soul*.

As you think about yourself as a soul, be intelligent and

patient with your own thoughts. Since human beings have created so many different concepts about souls throughout the ages, many of the present ideas about souls can be rather confusing and misleading.

To understand the nature of this confusion, imagine that you are with a friend of great beauty. You love your friend deeply. You are about to take a long journey without your friend, so you make a doll that looks like your friend. You want the doll to remind you of your friend's beauty while you are away.

While you are traveling, when you can no longer directly perceive your friend, you become so desperately lonely that you begin to imagine that the doll is actually your friend. You meet a person on your journey, show the person your doll, and say, "This is my friend."

Although you truly believe that the doll is actually your friend, in truth, the doll only resembles your friend. There is a certain correspondence between the two realities—the doll and your friend—but the doll is not the *truth* of your friend. It is a *symbol* for the reality that is your friend. In your confusion you have mistaken a symbol for truth. Thus, not only have you distorted your own perceptions, but you have also unintentionally misled the person to whom you showed your doll.

Through all periods of human life in physical form, certain human beings have inwardly experienced the reality of their soul. As those human beings communicated their inner experiences to others, their own personality patterns—their thoughts, feelings, beliefs, attitudes—influenced their communication. Thus, through the ages these human representations of souls have been *personal constructions*, based upon inner experience but *created* by human personalities. Such human communications about souls are similar to the doll of your friend. Just as the doll has a certain similarity to your friend, the human communications have a certain correspondence to the direct experience that the human beings had of the soul. But the communication is not the truth of the soul, just as the doll is not the truth of your friend. And depending upon the skill of the dollmaker, the doll can be either a fairly accurate representation of your friend or it can be highly distorted. In the same way human concepts about the soul can be relatively accurate or greatly distorted, depending upon the human beings who created them.

Regardless of their accuracy, the teachings and writings of human beings who have attempted to communicate about the soul through the ages can be seen as "dolls" of the soul. They are *human-created images*. They are representations that have been colored by the personality experiences of the human beings who have created them. They are not the truth of the soul. As human beings have mistaken their own creations for the truth, they have not only confused themselves, but they have unintentionally misled those to whom they have communicated as well.

As you now stand beyond your human life in your *true* form as a soul, you are quite a different being from what you presently experience yourself to be in human life. However, if you try to imagine your soul existence from the human point of view, your creation will be colored by your personality thoughts, feelings, and beliefs, and you will tend to project your human limitations upon your soul. You will believe that beyond the stream of human life you carry your shoes in your hand. You will believe that your soul is constrained by the same narrow realities within which you presently live as a human being. The true majesty of your existence as a soul will elude you.

To look beyond the limitations of the physical world in order to clearly perceive your soul, it is beneficial to have a new way of seeing. With a new way of seeing, you can learn to expand your awareness so that you can travel beyond the narrow human perspective and gain a vision of life that reveals what is temporarily hidden behind the physical reality.

To expand your awareness, you can draw upon an ability that you already have within yourself to actually perceive your soul. That ability is not normally used in your daily life because you do not know that you have it. By patiently cultivating that ability and bringing it into the foreground of your awareness, you can become consciously aware of your existence as a soul.

You can begin to prepare the way for opening this inner ability by simply stimulating your thinking about the truth of your being. You can remind yourself each day that even as you walk in human form, you have your true existence in your soul form. You can remind yourself that in your soul existence, you have a full conscious awareness of vast spiritual realities. You can tell yourself that even as you wade through the stream of human life, temporarily experiencing yourself as a physical human being with limited awareness, you can learn to expand your awareness to discover, beneath your human experience, your deep soul knowledge of vaster worlds.

An initial step toward your inner opening to spiritual realities is the establishment of a willingness to go beyond your own thinking, to go beyond your mind.

LIMITS OF THE MIND

For those who set out to discover their spiritual being, which exists in a realm that is not physical, one of the first obstacles to overcome is a preoccupation with the intellect. Since the mind is so important for success in the physical world, in this period of great preoccupation with physical reality there tends to be a widespread overemphasis upon rational thinking and intellectualizing in day-to-day life. This has brought about a general dampening of the inner intuitive abilities in many people, making it difficult for them to perceive the nonphysical realities of life.

Often, the feeling of *knowing* something is strong in you because you have *ideas* in your mind about an aspect of life. Yet at times the ideas that you have are a distant echo of the *truth* of what you are trying to understand. For example, if you have learned about France in school but have never visited that country, you have information in your mind, and you could say, "I *know* France." Yet if you visit the country, you will discover that you "know" very little. You have no *direct experience* of the *reality* of the country. You have only ideas and information in your mind. In the same way many people have differing ideas and concepts about the soul and the spiritual realities of life, but very few have an ongoing *experience* of such realities.

Yet since the spiritual realities of life are usually hidden from most human beings, as you begin to open to an understanding of yourself as a soul, at first all that you have to represent these invisible realms are the ideas and concepts that you hold in your mind. As long as you realize that your ideas and concepts about your spiritual being are not the *truth* of that being, but simply abstract representations, then you can productively use your ideas and concepts as a starting point in your work. It is then a matter of finding ways to move from the ideas to the direct experience. This involves a process of growth that will enable you to eventually go beyond the limits of the mind.

A PROCESS OF GROWTH

In terms of human evolution the present human awareness of reality is not yet fully "grown." Therefore, because of your human nature, you are temporarily caught in a relatively narrow vision of what actually exists in life. Thus, at first it may be difficult for you to perceive your soul. Yet there is a natural *inner process of growth* at work within you that, if encouraged by you in ways that will be described in later chapters, can eventually lead you to a clear vision of yourself as a soul.

To think symbolically about how this natural process of

growth within you can help you grow out of a limited vision of life, imagine that you are a small puppy. You desire to eat food from a bowl. As you do so, you are pushed aside by larger dogs. You have difficulty finding enough to eat. If you say, "This is terrible, I will never get enough to eat," you misunderstand the nature of yourself because of your immature vision. From your present perspective as a small dog, you do not realize that in time you will grow to be a large dog, and you will have the power to eat your fill of food.

As you begin an understanding of your spiritual being, keep in mind that in terms of your present sense of yourself, in some ways you are a small puppy. Your present thoughts and feelings about your spiritual nature may not now seem strong, or real enough to sustain you. But remember that there is the inner process of growth occurring naturally within you. In time, as you consciously encourage that growth, you will become a "large dog." You will become large enough inwardly to begin to feed yourself from the "bowl" of eternal energies that are available to you. There will come a larger *knowing* of the truth of you, and that will lead to deep, beautiful, fulfilling feelings of your true Self.

To begin to stimulate your inner process of growth, it will be helpful to expand your understanding of how you as a human being are presently connected to the spiritual realities of life. Without entering into the full complexity of spiritual realities, you can form a simple vision of yourself as a soul. That vision can serve as a catalyst for your inner opening.

YOUR EXISTENCE AS A SOUL

To come to the full truth about yourself, it is important to know who you are *beyond* your present human Self that is now living in the physical world. You need a clear vision of yourself as a soul.

Although it is not possible to capture the soul in human

words, you can use words and ideas to help you move toward a deeper understanding of yourself as a soul. The words can be a signpost to direct your inner experience toward a deep intuitive knowing of your soul within your own experience.

As you begin to form your ideas about your soul, remember that in human life, because of a constant preoccupation with physical sense perceptions, it might be difficult at first for you to clearly understand your nonphysical existence as a soul. You are used to defining your life, and the reality of the world, in terms of physical objects and your relationship to them. When you try to understand a reality, such as your soul, that has no physical form, you can often have difficulty.

Therefore, in approaching an understanding of yourself as a soul, it is wise to begin in a simple way that is easy to grasp. For now, as a starting point for your growth, you can begin with the following simple intellectual understanding of your soul. As you learn to open yourself more and more to the spiritual realities, you can expand your awareness beyond this intellectual understanding. You can open an *inner perceiving ability* that, eventually, will enable you to *verify* the existence of your soul through your own inner perceptions.

Begin by considering that your soul lives in a world *that does not exist within time and space*. Since it is difficult for the human mind to imagine a reality that is not contained in time and space, you can use something familiar, but *not* physical, as a reference point. You can initially think of the nonphysical reality of your soul as a vast, unending *experience*. Imagine an experience that has no limits, and that exists beyond time, space, and the physical universe.

You are already used to thinking of experience without reference to time and space. For example, when you have an experience of love, you do not ask, "How much space does this love occupy?" You do not ask, "Where is this feeling of love located?" You do not ask, "How much time does this feeling of love take?" You simply *experience* the love. You *feel* it. You *rejoice* in it.

Imagine that there is an indescribable *experience of love* that permeates all that is. Then imagine that in this love experience there is a magnificent being. That being is you as a soul, existing in a wonderful nonphysical realm, sharing an ongoing experience of love with many other beings.

This can be a starting point for your vision of yourself as a soul. However, truly understanding your soul requires a *creative* act that you can carry out within yourself, an act that can take you beyond your present limits of thinking. What you will try to creatively grasp is the *essence* of your soul, not the *form*. For example, imagine that you are thinking about your mother. To grasp the form of her, all that you need do is look at her body and her face. You can describe her form or even take a photograph of it. By so doing, you capture the *form* of a female human being. But you have not grasped the *essence* of your mother. You have not seized upon a personal experience of who your mother truly is.

To go beyond the mere form, you can see your mother as an individual human being who is unique in your life, and *who brings her inner intangible forces into your life in a way that personally affects you*. If you do that, then instead of a female human being, you now have a real mother. You have *created* a mother by *your inner responses to her essence*.

In a similar way, you can understand that your grasp of your soul depends upon the *feelings* about your soul that you are willing to *create* within yourself, not the perception of some form that you might attribute to your soul. If you try to feel within yourself that the energies of your soul are intangible forces of goodness, creativity, and love that are coming into you, then you are beginning to experience your soul in a way that is warm and personal. You are moving toward an experience of the essence of your soul, rather than trying to perceive the form of your soul.

It is as though you are trying to see an invisible person who is standing next to you. No matter how hard you strain your eyes, you will not see the form of that person. But if you say, "I will try to *feel* that invisible person loving me," then even though you cannot perceive the form, you can open your feelings and eventually feel the love as that invisible person shares its essence with you.

As you become more flexible in your thinking, *you can create certain new thought structures that will stimulate your intuitive ability to sense the existence of your soul.* To encourage this process, you can say to yourself each day:

> **"I will attempt to use words and thoughts in a broader and deeper way than I have ever used them. I will open to a brilliant new understanding within myself. As I do this, I will begin to open my intuitive capacities to actually perceive my soul as it exists beyond the physical reality."**

It is very important for you in your inner opening to know that there is a loving connection between your human Self and the forces of your soul. The love that joins you personally to your soul is powerful, uplifting, and wonderful. Imagining this love will help you begin to create feelings of being personally connected to the majesty of your soul.

If you think about your soul in a cold, abstract way, then you can create a feeling that the reality of your soul is impersonal and distant from you as an individual. To come closer to the truth, you can use your imagination to infuse your *feelings* into your understanding of the profoundly creative and loving existence of your soul.

For example, if you are listening to a beautiful symphony in an analytical, abstract way, you can say, "These are interesting sounds." You can measure the sounds of the various instruments, and you can study those sounds scientifically. That would bring you a certain intellectual knowledge, but it would not bring you much *feeling*. On the other hand, if you use your sensitivity, imagination, and heart to fully engage the beauty and the majesty of the music, you can literally enter into another dimension of reality beyond the intellectual—a dimension that is not cold and abstract, but is filled with energies of joy, purpose, and meaning. You can directly experience the deep truths in that musical dimension, truths that cannot be perceived through intellect alone. In a similar way, instead of simply thinking abstractly about your existence as a soul, you can learn to feel that the vast nonphysical forces of your soul are filled with beautiful realities that you can experience as harmony, creativity, and love. You can come to know that you, as a soul, are weaving your own energies into the wonderful symphony of life.

As you work with your personal opening, the inner process of growth that was described earlier will eventually lead you far beyond what you presently know about your soul. In time you can create feelings about your soul that go beyond present human language, symbols, and intellectual understanding. You can discover ways to grasp your soul that grow out of real inner experiences of truth, beauty, and love.

You can begin to stimulate the inner process of growth that will lead you to such experiences by understanding some important aspects of your growth and by learning how they are related to your movement toward your soul. You can also learn powerful ways to use your mind in the growth process. Both of these areas will be explored in the following chapter. That knowledge will help you build a solid foundation for your process of growth.

CHAPTER TWO

Your Process of Growth

———— ✳ ————

B ecause most people have not yet gained a full understanding of the reality of the soul, they often engage in
intellectual flights of fantasy about the soul. Such fantasies can be stimulating, and perhaps even lead to some
beneficial changes, but they do not usually lead to a direct
experience of the soul.

It is as though you would say, "I love driving," and each
day you drive your vehicle in circles. It is not bad to drive in
circles, you simply do not go anywhere. It would be more
productive to drive to a certain destination.

You can unintentionally create fantasies about your soul
that cause you to think in circles, going round and round
with ideas about the soul that are too small and too limited.
That is not bad, but it would serve you better to have a *direction*, a clear sense of how to move out of fantasies toward the
truth of your soul.

As you begin your movement toward an experience of
spiritual realities, you will be launching yourself into areas
that are not as clear and definable as the realities in the physical world. Thus, it is wise to have some guideposts or guiding principles to lead you in the right direction. Otherwise, it
is as though you are sailing a ship without a rudder. With
such a ship, you could not steer in a direction of your choosing. Your direction would be chosen for you by the wind and
the tide. In a similar manner, it might be possible for you to
make an opening to spiritual realities while holding confused ideas about your soul, but the subjective experiences

that you would have could be distorted by your confused thoughts and feelings as they interact with the spiritual forces of life. You would then have self-created fantasies about your soul, rather than true perceptions of your existence as a soul. That would not be bad, and you might even find it interesting, but it would not lead you where you wish to go. It would lead you wherever the winds and tides of human imagination carried your human consciousness.

In the inner process of growth that leads to a conscious awareness of your soul's existence beyond the physical reality, there are four areas of focus that can serve as a rudder to your ship, that can help you move in directions that will eventually allow you to arrive at a deep experience of your soul. You can understand these areas as four *pillars of growth* that can become the foundation for your direct experience of spiritual realities.

Working with these pillars of growth can help you use your mind in ways that will open your conscious awareness to the realities of your soul. These four areas can give direction and purpose to your voyage of discovery. Just as the table from which you eat must have four legs to be truly stable, the foundation for your search for your soul can rest solidly upon the following four pillars of growth.

THE FIRST PILLAR OF GROWTH

First of all, your growth toward an experience of your soul will depend upon *a willingness to trust in yourself*. This does not mean to trust in *your present thoughts, feelings, and beliefs*. They can be quite confusing and misleading. Instead, you will strive to trust that *within you* there is the most extraordinary being that you can imagine—a being larger than all of the ideals that you have ever had or thought about. You will learn to trust that you are much more magnificent than you have ever dared believe. Even in your most positive visions of yourself, you have not approached the fullness of your true inner magnificence.

As you begin to learn to trust that there is a most wonderful being within you, a being that is usually hidden beneath your conscious thoughts and feelings, it will be important to avoid the temptation to try to *prove* the existence of this aspect of yourself. Until you have learned to directly experience the spiritual realities, it will be difficult to prove that your inner magnificence is real. Thus, it is necessary to *trust* the truth of this as a beginning foundation for your growth.

This area of trust can help you be clear about who you truly are, particularly when you describe yourself in inaccurate ways in your own mind. For example, if you say, "I am unworthy," then if you are willing to trust that the truth is that you are a magnificent being, you can see that when you *feel* unworthy, you can say the truth to yourself in this way: "I am *temporarily feeling* unworthy. I am *permanently* a magnificent being." Whenever you have any limiting feelings or thoughts about your human personality, you can say, "I am *temporarily* this limited experience. I am *eternally* magnificent."

Imagine that you are feeling that you are a bad person. Trusting in yourself as a magnificent being, you ask, "Does this feeling of badness align with the truth of me?" You can see that badness is not a quality of your true eternal magnificence. Thus, you can say, "I am *not* a bad person. I am simply *temporarily* feeling bad about myself. The truth is that I am *eternally* a magnificent being." Gradually, you will learn to feel the difference between temporary human experiences and the larger truth of yourself.

Yet even though it is very important to grasp the magnificence of your eternal being, for the greatest growth in your life it is wise to also accept and honor your temporary human experience. You would not wish to ignore it in your spiritual pursuits. However, you do not need to accept a temporary human experience as the *truth* of your entire being. You can say:

> **"No matter what I am temporarily experiencing as a human being, I trust that the truth of my being is an extraordinary magnificence and goodness. It is a goodness that is more than I can possibly imagine while I am in human form."**

When you take this attitude toward yourself, you will begin to discover the truth about yourself. Aligning with that truth day by day will accelerate the process of growth toward a conscious awareness of your soul.

THE SECOND PILLAR OF GROWTH

The second pillar for your process of growth is *the willingness to know that negativity is a human creation*. You will need to understand that pain and suffering are created by human beings.

As negativity enters your thoughts and feelings, it stirs the darkest experiences that you have ever known. Even to think about negativity is frightening to some people. Because of this dramatic impact of negativity upon the human personality, many people have come to believe in the existence of negative forces in life that are outside human choice and control. Although this is an understandable response, it is far from the truth about life. (This issue will be addressed in further detail in Chapter Four.)

As you move toward an experience of spiritual realities, temporarily leaving behind the stabilizing aspects of your normal thoughts and feelings, it will be important to know and feel that all negativity is human created—that all negativity is *temporary*. To remember this, you can say to yourself each day:

> **"When I am having a negative experience in my daily life, I can expect it to seem quite real. That is the nature of human negativity. But I will always remind myself that all negativity is a human-created darkness that can only temporarily obscure the light of truth. In time all darkness must**

end. And the underlying magnificence of life will emerge through the momentary obscurity."

In the following chapter you will explore these aspects of negativity in greater detail. You will also learn how to recognize, and heal, the causes of your own negativity.

THE THIRD PILLAR OF GROWTH

The third pillar of your process of growth is *learning to perceive that you are connected to all living beings*. As a human being, it can be difficult to be aware of this connection. You can create a temporary experience of isolation and aloneness. If a beloved one dies, you can feel, "We are now separated forever." However, you can come to understand that these *appearances* of separation are a temporary human experience, not a truth. No matter what your temporary experience might be, you can remind yourself each day:

"I am joined to all living beings on earth, and beyond earth. This connection may be difficult for me to see at times, but it can never be broken. As I work patiently day by day to open my heart to others, I will feel my connections to others in a deeper, more beautiful way."

It can also be difficult for you to feel that you are connected to people who act in very negative ways, people whom you may even despise. If you see a person whom you hate, you might say, "Certainly, I am not connected to that terrible person." You can accept such thoughts and feelings as a *temporary experience*. You do not need to accept them as the truth. You can say to yourself, "If I am connected to all living beings, then this person whom I hate cannot be an exception." In time, with the inner openings that you will make, you can discover that the *soul* of that person is connected to your own soul in very deep ways. You will also discover strong, invisible *energies* of creativity and love that connect you to all human beings, including the person whom you hate.

Such connections may be difficult to truly feel at this time, but you can *think* about them. Thinking about being joined to all living beings is the first step toward actually feeling and perceiving that connection. (This will be explored more fully in Chapter Four.)

THE FOURTH PILLAR OF GROWTH

The fourth pillar of growth is difficult to put into words, for each person has different, often contradictory thoughts and feelings concerning this area. To establish an understanding of this area, you can think in terms of what you choose as your primary spiritual focus in life.

The most powerful spiritual focus for a human being is one that includes *all* of life, without limit, without human distortion. This understanding can guide you in your choice of what you will dedicate yourself to in your quest for an experience of spiritual realities—what you will honor, venerate, and worship in your life.

In seeking the "highest" spiritual focal point to which to dedicate yourself, the idea of *God* might be the most convenient structure for your mind and emotions. You can say, "The largest possible goodness that I can imagine, I will call God. That is the highest spiritual focus in my life, and I dedicate myself to that." This does not mean that you know exactly what God is. You are simply using the idea of God as a reference point to think about the largest goodness in life.

You are free to call this goodness the Buddha, you can call it the Christ, you can think of it as your Higher Being, you can symbolize it in any way that pleases you. However you might choose to think about God, for the present, until you have learned to consciously penetrate the spiritual realities, you can express the fourth pillar of growth to yourself in this way:

"I am awash in the radiance of God (Buddha, Christ, my Higher Being). I am bathing in the unending spiritual forces of goodness and love that constantly pour into me, nurture me, and bring the very life into my body, the divine spark into my existence as an eternal being. I am literally floating in this love, this perfection, this goodness, and I am never apart from it."

Again, this may be difficult to actually feel at times, but you can *think* it whenever it pleases you. Each day you can practice using your mind to turn your awareness to this truth. As you shall see, the intelligent use of your mind to think such thoughts of truth will be a powerful factor in your process of growth. You can also use your mind in the following ways to help build a beautiful structure of spiritual experience upon the four pillars of growth.

YOUR MIND AND GROWTH

Because you are focused primarily upon the physical world, you will normally use your mind to perceive only a very narrow range of reality. Many people will unintentionally narrow their range of perception even more by limiting their curiosity and growth, and by constantly emphasizing less important aspects of life. By failing to be creative and vigorous in life, and by refusing to search for a larger experience of life, they seriously limit the way in which they use their mental capacities.

You can work with yourself each day to use your mind to stimulate the process of growth and to expand your conscious awareness. Here is how you can accelerate your growth by using your mind in three areas.

First, you can continually stimulate your desire to know more about every aspect of life, constantly looking beneath the surface of all experiences.

You can look for new ways to see, understand, think, and feel. You can lovingly encourage yourself to expand in these areas. Each day you can set yourself certain tasks to carry out in your ordinary affairs that will encourage you to expand. For example, you might decide that in communicating with people in the workplace, you will pay more attention to them, try to feel them more deeply, and be more sensitive to them. This will help you penetrate the superficial level of your relationships to reach a deeper experience. Such tasks can be created in all areas of your life in which you desire to use your mind—your creative thinking—to stimulate more growth.

Second, you can pay attention to old habits that limit you, identify those habits, and then change them.

For example, if you wake up each morning thinking and feeling, "I am so confused about my life, I have no purpose in my life," then you are using your mind to continue habits that convince you that you cannot fulfill yourself. These are *thoughts* and *feelings*, not the *truth* about your life. However, by habitually feeding such thoughts and feelings to yourself, you are using the power of your mind to convince yourself that there truly is no purpose to your life. This causes you to see in your day-to-day life only that which "proves" your negative conclusions about yourself, and your negative attitudes become a more deeply ingrained habit.

You can become aware of such habits by asking yourself each day, "How am I using my mind? What are the primary conclusions that I draw about myself and my life? How do these conclusions affect my life?" If you see that they are limiting, you can say, "I am using my mind to narrow my range of awareness. I will not find a broader truth if I constantly repeat this same habit." You then learn what the habits are, you understand them, experience the negative thoughts and feelings in them without pushing them away, live through the negativity, heal it, and dissolve the habit. (In Chapter Three you will learn how to heal negativity.)

The third, and most important, area of work in using your mind to stimulate growth is the reenvisioning of yourself, but it would not serve you without the first two areas.

This means that you can create new thoughts and ideas about who you are and what your mind is. You can do this by focusing upon some of the larger visions of yourself that have been presented in the previous chapter and in this one. You can remind yourself often:

"I am not my human mind. I am part of a larger reality. But temporarily, I am understanding that larger reality with my mind. So I will need to feed my mind larger thoughts and feelings in order to stimulate it to reflect the larger realities."

You can think quite often about your spiritual nature, about the large, magnificent reality of you as a soul. Each day you can remind yourself:

"Even though I may not always consciously perceive the forces of my soul, those forces are the underlying, ongoing truth of my life. Even if I cannot feel this truth at all times, at least I can use my mind to remind myself that I am a magnificent soul. If I cannot always perceive my existence as a soul, at least I can use the power of my mind to think about that existence."

As you work with your mind each day, remember that your conscious thoughts have certain inherent human limits. To remain aware of this, it is wise to say to yourself each day:

"My thoughts can be very important to me while I am temporarily expressing in human form. I need to accept my thoughts and consider them seriously in order to decide if they are benefiting or confusing me. But I do not need to believe that my human thoughts are the truth about life. At times my thoughts may reflect truth, but I need to be clear that human thoughts are not truth. They are only human thoughts, and they are constantly changing throughout my lifetime."

You can use your mind to grow in profound ways, and to master life on earth more and more in this lifetime and in preparation for future human lifetimes. To remember this potential, each day you can say to yourself:

> **"I rejoice that I can live my present human lifetime with a mind of great strength and creativity. Of course, I desire to use my mind perfectly, and perhaps I shall in a future time. But for now it is exhilarating simply to have the opportunity to be alive in human form, to use my mind to be a part of the incredible symphony of human life, and to bring forth the music of my soul forces through my own human instrument, which includes my mind, my feelings, and my self-awareness."**

Working patiently with your mind, you will learn to make a gentle silence within yourself, during which you can begin to feel the loving forces of your own soul penetrating you. You can allow yourself to feel a marvelous sense of celebration of yourself as a human being who is bringing mind, emotion, and the forces of your soul together in a beautiful human expression.

In order to begin such an opening within yourself, it will be necessary to look closely at the *limits* that presently exist in your personality which can prevent you from opening. These limits are the negative thoughts and feelings that arise in your daily experience. To make a full opening to the magnificence of your soul, it will be important to understand your human negativity and to know how to heal it. Therefore, the next important step in your growth process is to take a closer look at human negativity and to learn ways to master it in your day-to-day life.

CHAPTER THREE

Transforming Negativity

———— ✳ ————

As you begin to expand your awareness to prepare to enter the spiritual dimensions of life, you will be setting out upon a pathway that is different from what you might be used to in your pursuit of accomplishments in the physical world. In mastering the physical world, with its tangible challenges and burdens, you usually bring your forcefulness and will to bear upon a task in order to manipulate all of the factors until you eliminate obstacles and achieve the desired result. Learning to experience spiritual realities is not a process of forcefully eliminating obstacles to achieve a *result*. It is more a matter of *creatively adjusting your inner life* in order to achieve a new kind of *experience*. It is not a process of *doing*. It is a matter of *being*. You will learn a new, deeper way of being yourself.

Being yourself in an expanded way involves a sequence of delicate inner adjustments that you will learn to make within your daily human experience. It involves *an inner opening of your whole personal Self.* Because your whole personality is involved in your spiritual opening, distortions in your thoughts, feelings, and beliefs can interfere with your intuitive abilities, making it difficult for you to have a deep spiritual experience. Therefore, before you begin to make the specific openings that are necessary to experience the forces of your soul, it is important to look at the factors in your personal Self that might interfere with your movement toward a deeper experience.

The greatest interference to your direct perception of

spiritual realities is *human-created negativity*. This is usually experienced as *fear* and *emotional pain*. Such experiences can affect your thinking patterns in a negative way. When your personality is caught in negativity, your inner perceptions are squeezed and numbed. You become so pressured by inner tension that you cannot calm yourself enough to be sensitive to the spiritual realities. Temporarily, your thoughts and feelings are overwhelmed by the intensity of human negative experience, and the more subtle spiritual realms are obscured. Therefore, before you can fully open yourself to the beauty of your soul, you will need to learn to free yourself from the distortions of fear and emotional pain.

This does not mean that you must be perfectly positive every moment of your life. It is not necessary to totally eliminate all fear and pain from your life in order to have a deep spiritual experience. You simply need to clearly understand how you create human negativity and then gain some experience in the healing of it.

To begin to work toward this, it is important to understand certain factors that have intensified human negativity at the present time on earth.

NEGATIVITY AND HUMAN COMMUNICATION

Many people believe that there is a *badness* in human life, and that there has always been badness. This belief is understandable, given the way human beings have chosen to communicate with one another in the public arena, particularly in the teaching of human history, and the communication about world events through news reporting.

The primary focus of this communication is usually on the dramatic events that drastically change people and nations. These are often quite negative events, such as war between nations, the struggles of one group against another, natural disasters, and violence. Therefore, in your own life, given your "training" in modern society, you can consider that it is quite "normal" for you to feel that there is badness in human life. Because much of what you have been taught through public communication has been so focused upon negativity, it can appear to you that negative events dominate both the past and the present.

To adjust to this distorted influence, you need to realize that negative events have been exaggerated in importance by communications about history and by news reporting. You can feel this by imagining that you are looking at a field of cows. You see one white cow, and the rest are black. You are very frightened of white cows. You ask, "Why is this white cow with the black ones?" You become consumed by that question, so you begin to specialize in the study of white cows. Eventually, you begin to believe that white cows are more important than black ones, even though only one white cow is in the field. Because of your fear, *you have made the smaller reality more important than the larger one*.

As human beings have been taught about negativity through the present study of history and through the communication media, a feeling that negativity is very important has been created. This is stimulated by the human fear of negativity, and the feeling that if negativity is constantly addressed, then perhaps it can be eliminated. This focus on the negative events of human life has obscured the fact that for thousands of years, billions of human beings have lived on the face of the earth creating love, warmth, friendship, and goodness in their day-to-day lives. So many human beings have loved one another and rejoiced in life. They have given one another kindness and consideration. They have created beauty and joy. However, since these simple daily human expressions do not usually change nations in a dramatic way, those who create human history do not focus on them. The generation after generation of human beings who have loved one another, and who have created their lives in kindness and goodness, are the many black cows in the field. The dramatic negative events are the single white cow.

Be aware that your response to life will tend to be exaggerated by this human preoccupation with negativity. You can avoid confusion in your inner work by being alert to this influence upon your attitudes, and by healing any negativity that grows out of it. If not healed, such a negative influence can lead you to feel that the true nature of human life is badness, pain, and suffering.

THE INTENSITY OF EMOTION

Another factor in the exaggeration of negativity is the intensity of the human emotional nature, along with the human tendency to respond quite dramatically to emotional pain. When you feel emotional pain, you feel it deeply and strongly, unless you have numbed your feelings. From the human point of view, pain is more dramatic than love and goodness because pain *threatens* you, motivating you to take some action to eliminate the threat. Under the impact of this perceived threat, your emotional patterns will often exaggerate the experience of pain.

You have had painful moments that, because of this emotional intensity, have registered quite deeply upon your feelings and your memory, creating a sense of importance associated with pain. The feeling that pain is very important, combined with your feelings of heaviness from the negativity of history and news reporting, can create a sense of darkness, threat, or danger in life. This magnifies your feelings of negativity even more, setting the stage for a preoccupation with negativity. In spite of all of the magnificence in life, under these influences you will tend to see only badness at certain times.

All of this can also be intensified by a feeling of badness about yourself personally. As you grow up in life, experiences with family, in school, and in society in general teach you how to find fault, how to criticize. Many people have become quite adept at criticizing, and they feel comfortable engaging in criticism. It becomes a habit that they eventually turn toward themselves. The result is usually the creation of an inner sense of badness or unworthiness about themselves.

By understanding these tendencies that can influence your personality toward negativity, by observing them, by working with them patiently and lovingly, and by adjusting your responses to them, you prepare yourself to enter into the healing of fear and emotional pain. You can gain a clarity and wisdom that will enable you to heal negativity with effectiveness and joy.

THE NATURE OF FEAR

The most distorting influence in human life is *fear*. You can begin your understanding of fear by considering that *fear is a temporary loss of confidence in life*. It usually comes with a feeling of, "Something bad is about to happen to me." The feeling of badness overshadows the true harmony of life, and, temporarily, you are unable to feel confident that there is any goodness in life.

To clarify this, imagine that you are an expert mountain climber. You are standing on the summit of a mountain and the wind is blowing very hard. Standing next to you is a friend who has no experience with climbing. You stand boldly in the wind, rejoicing in the beauty and freshness of the moment, feeling a *goodness* in life. Your friend stands in the same wind, on the same mountain, and is terrified of being blown off. Under the very same conditions, your friend feels a badness in life, and you feel a goodness. The difference is *a confidence in life*, brought about by your depth of *experience* and a trust in your *ability* that your friend does not have.

In your inner work it is beneficial to see fear as more than just a feeling of fright. The broadest and most helpful way to understand fear is to consider it to be any feeling of *badness* inside you, any feeling that would say, in effect, "There is no goodness in this moment. I am about to be blown off the mountain of life."

If a large tiger rushes toward you with its mouth open, you will have a feeling of fright. That is quite clearly fear. However, imagine that you have given yourself fully in a deep love relationship, and your beloved has a sexual liaison with someone else. You have a deep feeling of abandonment, betrayal, and pain. You might not describe this as fear, but there is a great feeling of badness in you that is related to a fear of loss of love. For your purposes of healing negativity, it is wise to think of any feeling of badness as fear. Fear can be any feeling that makes it hard for you to believe that there is goodness in life.

At this time there are many reasons why you might feel that goodness is not present in life. The constant reporting of negative events and potential physical dangers by the communication media can make you feel, "At any moment there might be a war, or poverty in my life, or I might contract a fatal disease, or we all might be destroyed by a nuclear holocaust." Because human imagination is so active and powerful, when you become caught up in fear, you can begin to see many things in life that can frighten you. Once you fall into the habit of believing that you are not safe, you can find many compelling reasons to believe that life is bad. By doing this, you unintentionally make fear and negative feelings your god. You bow down before them, so to speak, allowing them to reign over you.

Many people will desperately try to find pleasurable feelings to replace their feelings of fear. They will frantically pursue physical pleasures, such as sexual fulfillment, or become preoccupied with career, love affairs, or family complexities as a way of distracting themselves from the fear. There can be creative, beneficial reasons for pursuing joy in these areas; however, at times the pursuit is mixed with a feeling of desperation and a desire to escape the fears of life. Many people will feel, "I must do something immediately to bring some joy, some fulfillment, some sense of stability, or I will be overcome by pain and suffering."

What many are now discovering is that a desperate pursuit of pleasure in an attempt to escape pain and suffering does not bring fulfillment. It does not bring the true joy that you are seeking. It does not bring truth to your moment or stability to your life. It simply hides your fears for a while. The true stability comes when you can convince your personality that *you cannot be damaged or destroyed by what you fear*.

If you are the expert climber who has lived through so much in climbing many mountains, you are quite certain that the wind will not blow you off the mountain. Your stability is rooted in the confidence that comes from your experience with mountains. So it is in your human experience of life on earth. You can learn to feel how much experience you have gained in living through many human lifetimes in the past. You have suffered in many ways in the past. You have been physically damaged in your body, and you have even died in many bodies. Yet you continue to exist in this moment, undamaged by any past pain and suffering. As you open your inner awareness more and more, you will come to know that *you will never be damaged by any experience in life or death*. You are an *eternal* being. And from your many experiences in many past human lifetimes, you are also a master of human life, whether you can presently feel it or not.

If you *can* feel day by day that you are a master of life, you can stand boldly on the mountaintop of human life and dare the winds of challenge to blow, savoring the opportunity to test your skills against all aspects of life, bringing your strength, courage, and power to bear upon complex life situations. At times you might suffer, but you can work with any feelings of pain and suffering, and you can heal them. You can *know*, as you face each challenge, "This challenge might be painful, but it is temporary."

Fear is a *human-created* experience. It is created by distorted human thinking and feeling. It can be accelerated by harsh experiences in the outer world. It can be stimulated by dangerous situations in life. It can be intensified by poverty, loneliness, hunger, and many human challenges. However, fear is always *temporary*. You have within you the powerful forces of your soul, and of God itself, to use in the healing and mastery of your fear.

Fear can manifest itself in your emotional life in a number of ways. By understanding more about each of the following negative feelings and how to heal them, you can prepare the way for transforming the inner blockages to your deep experience of spiritual realities.

FEELINGS OF UNWORTHINESS

Often, the fear and negativity in your emotional life can manifest themselves as feelings within you that say, "I am unworthy, I am not a good person." Such feelings are a result of not seeing the true goodness of yourself because of distorted attitudes.

As you work with feelings of unworthiness, your first challenge is to convince yourself that such distorted attitudes are not the *truth* about you. They are simply *feelings* that you have learned to create about yourself. The truth is that beneath your feelings of unworthiness there are always the ongoing, nonphysical energies of your true being—the forces of your soul—that animate your self-awareness and make it possible for you to think and feel.

Any feelings of unworthiness need to be *accepted* by you, just as all challenging feelings need to be accepted. When you have such feelings, you can honestly say, "Today I feel unworthy. I feel as though I am a miserable person. But my challenge is not the fact that I *have* these feelings of unworthiness. My challenge is that in the past I have believed that these feelings are the truth about me. Now I invite these feelings forward to be fully experienced. I enter these feelings. I might share them with a friend. I will explore these feelings, experience them deeply, vent them, and then remind myself that these are feelings, not the truth about me."

After you have explored the feelings of unworthiness, it is important to say the truth to yourself. You might say it in this way:

"I have just lived through feelings of unworthiness that have come from a distorted attitude toward myself. The truth is that I am a magnificent human being with many wonderful qualities."

As you vent your feelings of unworthiness, you will heal them. As you return to thoughts and feelings of the truth of yourself, you will heal the distorted attitudes that caused the feelings of unworthiness.

At times you might believe that in order to feel more worthy, you must discover *why* you feel unworthy. You might feel that you must discover who wounded you and molded you in a distorted way. You might believe that you must find someone to blame for what you feel to be the badness within you. Such work might be interesting, and you may learn something about your personality, but it will not usually be inspiring or healing. It is often more beneficial to say:

"No matter what may be the cause of my feelings of unworthiness, from this lifetime or from my past lifetimes, at this point I simply have a habit of creating the feelings of unworthiness. I accept that. I accept the feelings, and I will work with them until I know that they are feelings, not truth. Then I will release the habit of feeling unworthy."

Many people who struggle with feelings of unworthiness will overcompensate for them by attempting to accomplish great things in life in order to prove to themselves and others that they are worthy. At times this might be beneficial. However, the person will usually know that the feelings of unworthiness are still there, no matter what great accomplishments they achieve. The feelings of unworthiness have not been brought into the daily experience to be fully lived through, released, and healed.

In your movement toward truth in this lifetime, one of your primary blockages will be patterns of self-diminishment that you create through inner criticism and fault finding. Such patterns not only distort your perception of your true goodness, but also temporarily cripple your full potential as a human being. It is as though you have beautiful feet, but as you look at them, your vision is distorted, and you say, "What ugly feet. I cannot stand these ugly feet. I will cut them off." Then, after you cut off your feet, you say, "How terrible. Now I cannot walk. I want my feet back."

By misguided impulses within you that have caused you to overemphasize negativity that you believe you see in your personality, you have created self-defeating attitudes that at times have cut off the "feet" of your personality—your self-confidence, which is your base of personal stability. Then you find that you cannot balance yourself in harmony and joy. However, unlike your physical feet, your emotional feet can be sewn back on. All that you need do is recognize what you have inadvertently done and then change it. You can say to yourself, "By my self-criticism and fault finding, by creating feelings of inadequacy and unworthiness, I have cut the very foundation from under my human expression. I will now heal those old distorted patterns, and I will step forward into the joy and love that I desire in my life."

By healing your patterns of self-diminishment, you are putting your feet back on. You are removing the blockage that prevented you from discovering the foundation of many talents and abilities that you stand upon in this lifetime.

When you find yourself returning to some of the old habits of self-diminishment, you can say to yourself:

"I will now sew my feet back on. No matter what thought or feeling I may be having in this moment that says I am unworthy, I now turn the power of my thoughts and feelings to the truth. The truth is that I am a magnificent human being. The truth is that I am a beautiful eternal soul."

As you continue your loving work with yourself each day, you will come to know, without doubt, that there is a magnificence within you. You will feel it in the love, and in the feelings of goodness and beauty that you experience. And you will walk forward on feet of great strength and beauty throughout this lifetime.

FEELINGS OF REJECTION

Another challenging manifestation of fear as negative emotion can be experienced as the feeling of being rejected by someone. This is usually stirred up most intensely when you love another person who does not return your love in the way that you desire or does not love you at all.

In such cases you are dealing with the frustration of interrupted desire fulfillment. It is so important to you to fulfill your desire to be accepted and loved that when the fulfillment of that desire is frustrated, it can be quite painful. Before you begin to work with the feeling of pain from being rejected, it is wise to try to create some *fulfillment* in your life so that you can diminish the frustration. In other words, you need some experiences of being accepted by someone important to you. You can find someone—a friend, a family member, or even a counselor—go to him or her and say, "I desire to heal my pain of rejection, but first I need you to comfort me. I need you to remind me that I am a person who is lovable. I need to feel accepted and understood." This is a beneficial first step to take when you are suffering from the pain of rejection.

Next, gently remind yourself that this pain is quite understandable because all human beings so deeply desire to be loved that they will feel pain when they are rejected. In other words, you need to convince yourself that your feelings of pain are not an inappropriate response to the situation. They are a "natural" way to respond to rejection. You can say to yourself, "I need to have this feeling of pain for a while, not frantically rush around trying to make the pain go away by getting back the person who rejected me." You can remind yourself, "If I do not feel pain at being rejected, it means that I am hardening my heart, I am numbing my feelings. The fact that I feel such pain means that I have the courage to feel and to care deeply. I need to be very gentle with myself as I experience the pain."

Feelings of rejection require a very delicate touch. Resist the temptation to quickly push them away or hide them. You can even control the urge to rush ahead in your healing work. Give the painful feelings enough time to be fully experienced, and expressed to someone, so that they can naturally run their course. You will decide for yourself how much time is appropriate. Remind yourself, "If I cut short my suffering from the rejection, I will tend to bottle up some negative feelings that need to see the light of day, that I need to feel and communicate to others."

After you believe that you have experienced and communicated the negative feelings of rejection enough, the next step is to regain the feeling of your own magnificence. If you desire, you can try to communicate with the one who rejected you, attempting to reestablish a loving relationship that can help you feel you are indeed lovable.

If that is not possible, if the person does not wish to continue a relationship with you, then you will need to work to *release* the person and continue to heal your feelings of loss. There is no magical way to create harmony in such a situation, for it is clear that you cannot have the person you desire. But you can say to yourself, "I now must learn to live with the fact that I cannot be with this person at this time." You do not do this by hardening your heart or becoming cold inside. You do it by becoming even softer, saying to yourself, "I refuse to quit loving simply because this relationship has been painful."

You can love the person from a distance. You can send the person your love in your thoughts and feelings. However, at the same time it is wise to try to *diminish your need to be with the person*. This is a difficult task, but if you work patiently toward releasing the need, you will be moving toward freedom. You can say to yourself, "I love, I desire, and I need this person, but I cannot have a relationship with this person, so I must move forward in my life." Whatever it takes, try to gently release your need for the person *without hardening your heart*.

The next step is to turn your attention toward other people. You will learn that you can achieve your desired fulfillment with someone else. At first this may seem difficult, for you most likely created a feeling about the past person that would say, "This is the most desirable person in the world. There is no one else whom I can love as deeply as I love this one. This one is unique and special." Of course, these are *thoughts and feelings* that you have created. They are not the truth about life. In time you can open yourself to others, see *their* beauty and goodness, and you will find that you will create a deep, loving relationship with someone who truly desires to be with you.

FEELINGS OF SADNESS

Another way fear manifests itself as negative emotions is through feelings of sadness. Feelings of sadness are primarily related to your emotional intensity in life. It is like the pain of stepping on stones in the road when you are walking barefoot. Whether you step on a great number of stones or a few—whether you have a bit of sadness in life or a great deal—will depend upon several factors related to emotional intensity.

First, it depends upon whether or not you are in a hurry. If you are running down the road to reach your destination quickly, you are more likely to step on some stones. In other words, the more *passionate* you are in this lifetime, the more willing you are to feel intensely, the more you will tend to rush ahead in your life seeking strong fulfillment. With such an approach you will usually experience more sadness because of your emotional intensity. You will not always make the clearest, most thought-out choices. However, you will often receive your joy more quickly and intensely than someone who thinks and plans too carefully.

If you have this kind of passionate personality, it is wise to say to yourself, "My nature is to be passionate and intense, with a bit of impatience. I rush in where angels fear to tread. Therefore, I must simply accept sadness as a part of my life. It comes and it goes. I refuse to swallow my passion simply to avoid some feelings of sadness. I do not wish to walk slowly upon this path of fulfillment. I desire to rush forward." With such a personality you simply adjust for your intensity, and you resign yourself to more frequent bouts of sadness. You will adapt to them and learn how to live through them without so much pain.

If you are one who walks down the road of life with moderation, watching out for the rocks and trying to avoid them, you may only step on a few. In other words, you will make reasoned, balanced choices in your life—about relationships, career, money, about everything you do. You will take your time and be patient. With this approach you can have more feelings of harmony. It might take you longer to achieve intense fulfillment, but you will work at it steadily and patiently. There will most likely be fewer disappointments and less chaos for you. You will feel more steady inside. And you will tend to be less sad.

Those who walk the pathway of life at an extremely slow pace, who are always cautious, never take risks, and plan everything, will usually feel relatively even in their emotional life. Their pathway will not usually be bumpy. Usually exercising control over their emotions, they will not feel much passion or strong emotion. They will usually not feel a great deal of sadness because they do not feel anything in a strong way.

These are *generalizations* about different approaches to life on an ordinary, day-to-day basis, when there are no difficult challenges in your life. Although these generalizations will not apply to all individuals, they can help you understand the *consequences* associated with different approaches that you can take to your life. In general, if you are very passionate, the consequence will be more intensity in all feelings, joyful and sad. The more controlled you are, the less sadness, perhaps, but also less joy. It is not necessary that either approach be considered good or bad. Simply decide which one pleases you in your life. You are free to experiment with different approaches at different moments.

However, when the challenges of life begin to impinge upon you, many factors can temporarily "impose" experiences of sadness upon you. Most human lives have certain challenges. If you believe that challenge is bad, then you will have a great deal of sadness because you will have a great deal of fear that you are not safe. Thus, you will tend to be sad quite often, no matter what your personality choice might be, whether it is passionate, moderate, or controlled. If you can learn that challenges are temporary, you might have *some* sadness, but it will not last very long because you will find ways to heal it.

At times sadness is an expected *natural* response to life. If a beloved one dies, you will naturally experience sadness. If you did not feel sad, it would be an unusual response.

When *events* in your life bring on feelings of sadness, say to yourself, "Sadness is expected here. My challenge is to live through it with as much honesty and courage as I can, and to try to comfort myself with the love of others."

If you find that you are *constantly* sad, even when there is no challenge facing you, that is not a natural response. It means that you have become preoccupied with your own negative feelings. This usually occurs when you are isolated from others. This isolation could come about because you are not paying attention to other people, not opening to them, or because you have physically withdrawn from others and do not have enough opportunity to interact with them. The result is that you wrap yourself in your own negativity and it grows stronger and stronger. When there is no inspiration or love from other people coming into your inner experience, an exaggerated focus on your negative feelings can grow out of proportion and you can temporarily lose touch with the love and joy in life. In such a case you can address the isolation, disengage from it, and return your attention to strong, meaningful, loving relationships with others.

FEELINGS OF DEPRESSION

Fear can often be manifested as feelings of depression, meaning very deep or persistent feelings of despair, terribleness, or badness. Feelings of depression are a kind of intensification of sadness, multiplied by self-preoccupation. Such feelings can be associated with frightening or painful events in life, but prolonged depression is a matter of *losing yourself in your negative feelings*. This creates a temporary inner darkness that can appear to swallow you and all of life. In such experiences the illusion is that goodness has completely vanished from life.

At times you can unknowingly create feelings of depression as a kind of cocoon into which you withdraw in order to escape the pressures of your day-to-day life. It seems easier to simply give up and feel depressed than to face the challenges that seem so oppressive. If you can become aware of such a response, you can create a more positive cocoon. In other words, you can give yourself permission to temporarily withdraw from the challenge, rest and strengthen yourself, gain some understanding and insight into the problem, perhaps seek aid and encouragement from others, then return rejuvenated and heal the challenge.

At times prolonged feelings of depression can trigger certain abnormal chemical-electrical responses in the brain that can challenge your body. These abnormal responses can intensify certain nerve reactions throughout the body, but particularly in the spine and heart area. This can slow the circulation of the blood, reducing glandular responses, which interferes with hormonal functioning. This physiological response can create an added sense of heaviness and pressure, thereby frightening you more. It can cause a deepening of the cycle of depression. In such an instance it is very important to begin a healing process and regain your inner and outer balance in life.

If the depression is not severe, the key to healing it is to try to rise up out of your despair, go to others, and ask if they will comfort you and help you communicate your negative feelings. Then it is important to try to spend some time *giving to others*, helping them, trying to uplift them. This will draw your attention away from yourself and your preoccupation with your own negative feelings.

If your depression continues and deepens, you may need the help of someone with an expert knowledge of psychological processes. Human intensity is so great, mentally and emotionally, that if you establish a circular feeding of negativity to your emotions, to your brain, back to your emotions, back to your brain, round and round, at times the illusion of badness created by this can become so great that you can convince yourself that you are completely helpless. You can come to believe that you will never extricate yourself from the badness.

If you did not become terrified in your despair, eventually

your inner intuitive wisdom would guide you toward a natural healing of depression. But terrible feelings of depression are a large burden to bear. Therefore, it is wise to say, "I will not bear these feelings alone. I will go to someone and receive help in healing this temporary emotional distortion that I have created."

FEELINGS OF LONELINESS

When fear manifests itself as feelings of loneliness, there is usually a lack of fulfillment in your relationships with others, whether in love, friendship, or family. Feelings of loneliness are not particularly difficult to heal. You can simply let the feelings of loneliness prod you to rise up, go out into the world, and use your abilities to deepen your relationships. You can remind yourself:

> **"I am intelligent. I am creative. I am strong. I am lovable. I have the forces of my soul and of God inside me to draw upon to go forth into the world to create the relationships that I need to fulfill myself in love."**

To do this might be a bit frightening if you have withdrawn from relationships. Fears of others would have caused you to withdraw, so those fears can be stirred up when you seek to reengage others. Such fears *need* to come to the surface so that you may become aware of and heal them. Healing these fears will give you the confidence to share yourself with others so that you can create the deep relationships that will free you from the feelings of loneliness.

At times feelings of loneliness within you can arise when you continually direct harsh criticism toward other people. If you constantly find fault with other people, then even when you are with them you will find them uninteresting and not lovable. In this way you create a feeling that there is no one around for you to love. This, of course, is a distortion in your vision, and it creates a feeling of ongoing loneliness within you.

Constant criticism of others is usually related to a fear that you are unworthy. Unconsciously, you fear that if you let other people come close to you, they will see your unworthiness and condemn you for it. So inwardly, usually without noticing what you are doing, you adopt a habit of finding fault with others so that you can condemn them first. By criticizing them, you create the feeling that you do not want to be with them, which is an unconscious way to reject them and to hold them at a distance. If they cannot come close to you, then they cannot see what you believe is your unworthiness, so they cannot condemn you.

A frequent form of loneliness is that which is felt by people who are in love relationships, but who withdraw emotionally. They create a feeling of being distant and separate from the person they are with. They might extend this feeling to other people until they feel as if they are alone, even when they are surrounded by friends and loved ones. This is a more difficult area to heal. It requires persistent inner work with the negative feelings and a willingness to share the feelings with others.

Many individual mental and emotional patterns can cause a person to create an inner isolation. The most common one is the creation of a belief within yourself that you can never be complete in this lifetime. Usually, this comes about when you enter an area of life, particularly a love relationship, with great passion and enthusiasm, believing that the experience will magically fulfill you for a lifetime. After the initial enthusiasm wears off, and you again face your own fears and negative feelings, you feel deeply disappointed in love, or whatever you were pursuing. You may try a number of relationships, with the same result. You might turn to your career, or to the pursuit of wealth, but nothing heals the emptiness that you have created within your own feelings.

From experiences such as these, you begin to feel that life

itself is empty. You might feel, "I have tried so many ways to feel full and complete, but everything has failed me." You create such strong feelings of emptiness and loneliness within yourself that you begin to believe that loneliness is the true nature of life.

With such feelings of loneliness, as with other challenging feelings, you can begin your work by entering into the feelings and experiencing them deeply, and by communicating them to other people. Live through the feelings fully for short periods. At the end of that period of work, say the truth to yourself, whether you can fully believe it or not. You can say:

> **"These feelings of loneliness are not the truth about life. It is not true that life is empty. It is true that I have a feeling that life is empty. But this is a temporary feeling. I can heal this feeling. After I heal it, I will be able to feel the truth. The truth is that I am joined to so many by a deep energy that I can feel as companionship, friendship, and love."**

Feelings of loneliness can be very distorting when you create them strongly and for a long period of time. The emptiness can seem very real when you are caught up in it. Therefore, it will be important to continually work to accept the feelings of loneliness, live through them, communicate them, release them, and find the truth beneath them.

FEELINGS OF ANGER

As you try to understand and work with feelings of anger, the first step is to realize that anger is often a smoke screen for fears, using fear in the broad sense to mean any kind of feeling of *badness*. You will often *unconsciously* create feelings of anger when you are frightened, or feel badness, in order to avoid the pain of your fear. In other words, you displace the true cause of your distress, which is fear, and you unconsciously invent another feeling, anger, that usually helps you feel strong and powerful. Feeling angry and strong helps you maintain your acceptable self-image, while fear would lead to feelings of weakness and helplessness. Most angry responses are an unconscious attempt of your personality to maintain the illusion that you are not fearing badness in some area of your life, so that you can continue to feel powerful.

Those with a *chronic* problem of anger usually feel particularly small and helpless. Such feelings of smallness are so disturbing to them that it becomes very important to avoid the feelings. They will readily translate their feelings of helplessness into anger in order to feel more powerful. They do this unconsciously. When they can attack with their anger and cause other people to cower and withdraw, they feel quite potent. Even if their anger consciously displeases them, unconsciously a part of them decides that anger is preferable to feelings of smallness and helplessness.

Because anger is so strong and goes so deep, it requires courage to work with such feelings. You will need the courage to *have* the feelings and experience them, which is particularly difficult when you decide that your goal is to *eliminate* feelings of anger. For example, you may be striving to be a patient, kind person. Feelings of anger make you think that you are failing, so you will tend to swallow your anger or hide it. It will take courage to fully experience the feelings of anger inside you.

Next, you will need patience. It will require patience to let the angry feelings run their course so that you can calm yourself enough to communicate with others about your feelings of anger. It is not usually wise to try to talk about your angry feelings while you are dominated by them. Give them time to subside, then talk about them.

If you are angry with someone, after you have calmed yourself it is very beneficial to go to the person and ask for the person's *help*. You might say, "I am having some angry feelings and I need your help. I need you to listen to me. First, I will talk about my feelings—how it feels to be so angry. Then I need your help in working with the situation between us that I am angry about."

The next step is perhaps the most difficult. That is the task of discovering the fear that lives beneath the anger, to find out what the feelings of badness are that frighten you. If you are not aware of the fear, then you can learn to bring the hidden feelings of badness to your conscious awareness. You can say to yourself, "I have unknowingly stirred up feelings of anger to hide a fear from myself. What could that fear possibly be in this situation?" You can look deeply into your thoughts and feelings, trying to discover what feelings of badness are associated with your anger.

At times you can ask someone to help you discover what fears lie beneath your anger. For example, imagine that you have a spouse who is quite sloppy. Your house is very chaotic. You become angry about the messiness. In working to communicate with your spouse about this, you would first try to express, as calmly as possible, what you feel about the sloppiness. You might say, "The house seems so ugly to me. It feels bad to me to be in such an ugly house." Next, you would both try to discover why being in a sloppy house makes you feel so bad. You can ask yourself, "Why does sloppiness feel so terrible to me?" You can question yourself and search within for the hidden feeling of badness. Perhaps, in this example, you might discover that you have associated a sloppy house with people you have known in the past who were insensitive, unkind, and even violent. You feel that they were bad people. Living in a sloppy house makes you feel like them, and that seems bad and oppressive to you. Thus, your anger at your spouse arose out of your fear that you might be a bad person.

It may take time to find the fear beneath the anger, but you can eventually find it if you work patiently and lovingly with yourself. Then you can bring the feelings of fear to the surface. You can live through them, express them to others, and heal them. This will diminish the tendency to become angry in that particular area of your life.

You will still have your likes and dislikes in life, even after you heal fears that cause anger. In this example you may still dislike a sloppy house, even when you are no longer frightened that you might be a bad person. Then, without anger, you can say to your spouse, "Would you cooperate with me, for my benefit, and help me by creating neatness and order in our home?" After you have worked with your anger, you can ask others to work with you in areas of like and dislike, to help you feel more secure, steady, and fulfilled in the areas of your life that are important to you.

At times a bit of anger is simply a natural response to difficult life challenges. There may be some fears beneath the anger, but they may not be so persistent that you need to work with them. For most people, a bit of occasional anger does not need much work.

However, frequent uncontrolled anger can be a severe challenge to you and to those around you. It is wise to work diligently with such patterns to discover the hidden fears, and to heal them.

UNCOVERING HIDDEN FEARS

While you are in human form, it will be difficult to clearly know all aspects of your inner life. Your soul knows the complexity of you, but while you are human you can only partially understand your own complexity. You have agreed to live primarily on the surface of human life, not to see all of the secrets hidden beneath it. Usually, you will see only the narrow range of conscious experience that is necessary for the important accomplishments in your earth life. However, you can expand your understanding of your inner patterns if you wish to learn about hidden fears in you that need to be healed. Even though you have agreed not to have total clarity about your hidden patterns, you do have some freedom to learn more about them.

Your abilities to think, feel, and act are "tools" with which you can build a beautiful life or a miserable one. What will make the difference is the way you use those tools, the way you use your thoughts, emotions, and will. For example, if you use your thoughts to constantly say, "I am too poor, and I will always be poor," then your thoughts will create an experience of misery. On the other hand, if you say, "I have less money than I desire, but I have the ability to earn more," you can create a joyful life experience, even though you presently have less money than you desire.

The first step in uncovering your hidden fears is to ask yourself, "Where am I using the tools of my life—my thoughts, feelings, and will—to create such negative attitudes that they are making me miserable?" There you will find your fears. If you are using your thoughts and feelings to create a belief that you will always be poor, there is your fear. You are frightened of the pain and suffering that you associate with poverty.

Another way to reveal your hidden fear patterns is to ask yourself, "What do I believe is *bad* in life?" If you say, "I believe that it is bad when people are cold to one another," then you could say, "I have a fear of not being loved. I am afraid of people being cold and harsh toward me."

There are many ways to examine your personality patterns in order to find your fears. The starting point in your search can be feelings of badness of any kind. Whenever you feel, "This is bad," it is the doorway to underlying patterns of fear.

Remember that fear patterns can be deeply buried beneath many complex thoughts and feelings. Therefore, it is wise to take your time and be patient in working with them. It can help you a great deal to communicate your feelings to other people who are sincere and honest. This will help you reveal your fears by bringing your underlying feelings of badness to the surface.

However you decide to work with your fears, remind

yourself that negative feelings cannot harm you. Even if you *never* heal your fears in this lifetime, which would not be pleasant for you, your feelings of badness can only cause *temporary* pain. *They cannot damage your being.* Therefore, you do not need to be frightened of your negative feelings. You do not need to hide them. You can vent them by living through them and expressing them to others. You can say to yourself:

> **"Fear and pain are quite unpleasant. But the sooner I move toward such feelings, accept them, live through them, and heal them, the sooner I will return to my true purpose in this life, which is to manifest the joy and love that I have always desired."**

THE TRUTH ABOUT NEGATIVITY

As you work with negativity in your life, it is important to remember that while you live in human form not only do you feel, "I am my body," but you feel, "I am my personality." Therefore, whenever there is the negativity of pain caused to your body or your personality, that is a terrible event to you because the pain is filling all of what you believe you are—a body, a personality.

But you are only temporarily a physical body and human personality. You are always an eternal being. And even though pain and suffering can temporarily fill your human Self, such negativity cannot fill your soul. Pain may seem bad to your human Self, but as an eternal being you understand that pain and suffering are temporary experiences. You as a soul know that goodness has not disappeared from life simply because the human Self is temporarily experiencing negativity. Beneath the negative human experience of pain and suffering, hidden by that experience, there are the ongoing energies of eternal magnificence.

You as a soul understand that you have lived many human

lifetimes. In all of them you have had some human negativity. That negativity from your past human lives *no longer exists*. It has ended. *Any present negativity that you have will also end*. In time it will no longer exist.

It is also important to constantly remind yourself that *human negativity cannot damage you*. The things in life that cause pain and suffering can damage your *body*. But you are not your body, even though you may temporarily feel that you are.

These are the two important truths about negativity that you can say to yourself each day:

> **"Human negativity is temporary.**
> **Human negativity cannot damage my being."**

Hold these two truths in your mind as a basis for your unfoldment and growth each day. Remind yourself each day that fear, pain, and negative feelings are like dark clouds that obscure the sun. The clouds are *temporary*. They are eventually carried away by the wind. Behind them is the sun, which is permanent.

Your dark clouds of human negativity are quite temporary. They are always carried away by the winds of change and growth. Behind the clouds of negativity you can always find the permanent sun of love that is the force of God itself. This love is the truth of you. It is the force that pervades all of life. As you learn to feel this love, you open the door to greater fulfillment in all moments, and you prepare the way for a deep experience of your soul.

CHAPTER FOUR

Building a Foundation for Your Spiritual Breakthrough

---- ✳ ----

Once you begin to heal your negative mental and emotional patterns that block your awareness of the larger realities of life, you are ready to prepare a foundation for the inner work that will lead you to a direct experience of those realities. That foundation can best be built upon some important ideas and beliefs about the nature of spiritual realities and how they are experienced. You can learn to think in a broader way about certain aspects of spiritual attainment. You can create more enlightened attitudes that will help you move toward truth. Such enlightened attitudes can prepare the way for a deep experience of your soul.

THE NEED FOR ATTUNEMENT

Many people have already begun to follow an inner urge to know more of life. They have tried various methods of expanding their conscious awareness, such as meditation, contemplation, and prayer. At times these methods might be helpful, but too often they are practiced in a way that grows out of confused attitudes about the relationship between the human personality and the soul.

For example, even though many people are willing to believe that their soul has a perfection within it, they do not feel that perfection within themselves, so they come to believe that their soul is *separate* from their personality, or that there is a great distance between their personality and their soul. Therefore, when they use a method of meditation, they find themselves striving to close the gap, to cross the "distance" that they feel separates them from their soul. This creates an inner tension that makes it extremely difficult for them to relax enough to make the mental and emotional release that will allow them to expand their conscious awareness and perceive the spiritual realities. Thus, their meditation becomes an inner striving. There is no joy in it. They may even begin to dislike their periods of meditation and give up on them.

The truth is that there is no distance between your personality and your soul. The goodness of your soul lives *inside* your present human experience. It is simply hidden from your conscious awareness most of the time. You do not need to work to project yourself outside your personality in order to experience your soul. You need to expand your conscious awareness so that you can go deeper *within* yourself. To accomplish this, you can use a "method," but it is important to use one that is fresh and new, one that grows out of an inner joy, not an inner struggle; a method that leads you to truth, not to fantasies about spiritual realities.

In order to be free from any preconceived ideas that you may have about various meditation techniques, and to take a fresh look at the process of expanding your awareness to perceive spiritual realities, you can begin by using a new word to represent the method that you will use to experience spiritual realities. You can call your inner work an *attunement* to spiritual realities. By having a new word, you open the way for new meanings for that word. This can make it easier for you to come to a new *experience* when you are doing your inner work. You will be less likely to define your inner experience in terms of old, limited ideas and concepts.

You can consider that an *attunement* to spiritual realities is the *process* of inner work that you will do day after day to release yourself from the limited perceptions of ordinary reality and to expand your conscious awareness so that you can experience the spiritual realities of life. In your attunement you are not striving to go outside yourself and cross a gap to reach your soul. You are going *inward* to discover the beauty of your soul that already lives within you. You can use your attunement process as a way of temporarily disengaging from the overwhelming impact of your human experience in the physical world so that you can make that inward journey.

The human capacity to become passionate about something is very great. You can become passionate about anything—your work, a relationship, a hobby. You can also become passionate about discovering your eternal nature. If you turn your passion toward your attunement, then your attunement can become the way that you satisfy your desire to directly experience the spiritual realities of life.

LOVE AND ATTUNEMENT

As you begin to open to the spiritual realities, it is important to establish a feeling that you have a loving connection to those realities. If you do not create a feeling of personal love in your attunement, as you release your preoccupation with your physical life during the attunement period you can inadvertently establish a certain coldness and a sense of isolation. The release of daily human affairs, activities, and relationships that are familiar and comfortable to you can create a sort of inner vacuum in your personal experience of the moment.

For example, as some people try to conceive of what reality is like beyond the physical earth, under the influence of *science*, they may begin to imagine a cold, empty cosmos with uninhabited celestial bodies speeding about randomly in infinite space. Such an image could cause you to feel lost in a frightening, impersonal world. Therefore, in opening yourself to an experience of spiritual realities, as you begin to build your vision of what life is like beyond physical reality, it is wise to encourage a *personal* feeling of your spiritual nature—a feeling that your connection to the larger realities of life is rooted in a deep *love*.

As you begin to work with the attunement process in your daily life, it will also be important to make certain that you continue to develop loving relationships with other people around you. While you are alive in human form, you are free to choose to ignore other people and lose yourself in your personal affairs, giving all of your attention to the satisfaction of your own needs and desires. However, it may well be that when you come to the moment of your death, it will not matter so much to you how much you satisfied your personal needs in this lifetime, but rather *how fully you expressed the forces of your soul into earth in your relationships with the human beings about you*.

At times, because of confusion combined with your human intensity, you can unintentionally create the feeling that you are living alone on earth. You can feel that all that matters is what *you* think, feel, and do. You forget to fully use your capacity to extend yourself and share this earth life with others who, in time, you will discover are linked deeply with your own being. They are not separate and isolated from you. They are a part of you.

It is difficult for most people caught up in the complexity of the modern world, with its violence, chaos, and confusion, to be aware of the "energy of love" that constantly flows between all human beings. If you could become aware of this energy, you would realize that no matter how badly people might act toward one another, no matter how painful, frustrating, and frightening the physical world might seem to you at times, these temporary human challenges ride on top of a permanent love energy that connects you to all human beings. *Nothing in your physical life can diminish these energies of love.* They continue to connect you to others at every moment.

If you do not perceive these connecting energies of love in this lifetime, you can be assured that you will discover them after your death. However, it is much more joyful for you to discover them *before* you die. An awareness of this love can help you live a much more fulfilling and valuable life. Such an awareness can help you heal and forgive, for you can understand that these energies of love connect you even to your worst enemy. If you can learn to perceive this love bond, you can peel away all human distortions, fear, and misunderstanding, and you can discover that you and other human beings are eternal souls standing side by side in love.

If you make such an opening in your attitudes toward others, you will find that your relationships with other people will begin to deepen. You will feel more friendship and love in your day-to-day life. This can eventually lead to a deep feeling of meaningful, satisfying accomplishments in your relationships with others.

As you use your attunement process to deepen your experience of spiritual realities, it will be important to continue to create this openness to other people, for there might come a time when you experience such a great deal of joy and love in your attunement periods that your relationships with other people could seem less satisfying than your private inner experience. You might begin to indulge in your spiritual experiences in order to avoid other people, particularly if your relationships with others are difficult or painful.

Be aware that if you do not keep alive your feelings of love for others, you may begin to enter your spiritual experience as an escape from the challenges of human relationships. Such a choice could set the stage for using your attunement as an escape from all of the difficulties of life. You would soon forget that challenges can at times stimulate you to learn and grow in ways that joyful experiences cannot.

If you withdraw from other people and from challenges, your attunement could become an inner fantasy experience, based primarily on a desire for pleasure and self-indulgence, rather than a movement toward growth and truth. By keeping alive your love for other people, and by deepening your relationships with them, you invite balancing experiences into your life that will help you continue to grow as a human being, while you also pursue a deep experience of the spiritual realities.

GAINING TRUST

Another preparation for your spiritual breakthrough is to gain a deeper trust in your personal ability to attune to the truth of life. To accomplish this, first you can establish a commitment to perfection that is integrated with honesty about your thoughts and feelings. In other words, as mentioned in Chapter Two, you can learn to trust that there is a perfection in you and in life that is not limited or destroyed by any negativity that you might create with your human thoughts and feelings. You can come to trust that there is a goodness in all of life that cannot even be diminished by thoughts that temporarily cause you to believe that negativity is the underlying reality of human life on earth.

Each day you can work to feel and trust the inner perfection that lives in you. Yet at the same time you can try to honestly acknowledge anything that you think and feel that does not reflect that perfection. Thus, you might say to yourself, "Today I feel quite hateful. Everyone appears so ugly and repulsive to me." You do not need to try to eliminate those feelings simply because you are committed to the inner perfection. You can simply trust that *the perfection of you and of life continues to exist while you are having your negative feelings*.

After you accept your negative thoughts and feelings, remind yourself again that the negativity of human life is temporary. The more experience you have being honest with negative thoughts and feelings, and patiently living through them, the more you will come to know that they are temporary. Your movement toward perfection and the experience of spiritual realities is not a process of trying to force away your negative thoughts and feelings. It is a gentle, loving process of being honest about your negativity, living through it, learning about it, and eventually healing it.

This patience with negativity can also be taken into your attunement periods. If during your attunement you are attempting to feel spiritual truths, but instead you only notice a feeling of irritation about something in your daily life, it is not wise to rush to eliminate the feeling of irritation in order to become more spiritual. That only creates resistance and makes it more difficult to release the negativity. If you trust that the negativity is temporary, then you can notice it, accept it for a moment, and gently release it. You can also be willing to trust that the negativity does not diminish the perfection and goodness within you that you are attempting to experience in your attunement period.

As you learn to trust the goodness of life more and more, you can create moments in which you experience a wonderful openness and deep love in your attunement period. You can feel an expansiveness that becomes a kind of *holiness*—a feeling that life is truly precious and good. It does not matter what negative thoughts and feelings you have had during your day; in that moment of attunement in which you are willing to trust the underlying goodness of life, you can open the door to a wonderful inner experience.

RECEIVING GUIDANCE

Many who set out to attain a deep spiritual experience become interested in receiving *guidance* from spiritual realms. As you consider the issue of being "guided," it is important to be aware that it is a complex area that can be quite confusing.

Many people will ask, "How can I know the difference between my own thoughts and spiritual guidance?" There is no way to know this with *certainty*. That is because while you are in your present human form, you will perceive everything *through* your personality. Therefore, all spiritual guidance that you receive will be experienced through your humanness. If the "voice" of God itself spoke to you, you would hear it with your human ears, your human mind, your human heart. It would be filtered through your human subjectivity—your beliefs, attitudes, likes and dislikes. Therefore, in receiving guidance you can never be *certain* about what is spiritual truth and what is your own mind and emotions.

However, you can learn to feel an intensified *experience* of being guided. As long as you do not insist upon certainty, you can gradually begin to feel the difference between your "ordinary" experience of life and the moments in which you become consciously aware that you are receiving spiritual guidance.

To begin your understanding of this area, keep in mind the *constant* interplay between your human thoughts and feelings, and the spiritual forces of life that guide you. The forces of your own soul, the forces of guiding souls, and the forces of God constantly pour into you. Therefore, *there is never a moment in your life in which you are not receiving spiritual guidance*. But there are many moments in which you are not consciously aware of the guidance that you are receiving.

Although you are constantly receiving forces of guidance, *the guiding forces do not usually tell you what to do in the physical world, nor do they make your human choices for you*. The guiding spiritual forces inwardly urge you in directions that are important to your soul and to the harmonious unfoldment of life on earth. However, those forces do not interfere with your free will.

You are constantly being guided to open more, to feel life

more deeply, and to love more. However, you must *choose* to be receptive to these guiding impulses in order to bring them more fully into your day-to-day experience. In order to leave you free to choose, the guiding forces will not impose themselves upon you.

Usually, you are not aware of the inner impulses of guidance that flow into you because you are so busy pursuing your affairs in the physical world. However, at any moment you can choose to stop and create an inner silence, make your attunement, release the distractions of the physical world, and expand your thoughts and feelings so that they can be impressed by the spiritual forces. This might result in an inspired thought or feeling that is accompanied by a conscious awareness of the divine energies that are flowing into you. However, this usually comes along with an ongoing awareness of your ordinary thoughts and feelings. The guidance that impresses you inwardly does not usually overpower your ordinary experience. This means that your normal personality patterns will not be blotted out. Thus, if there are any strong distortions in your personality, they can affect your perceptions of guidance.

For example, imagine you are frightened that you will be poor throughout your lifetime. You decide to make an attunement and ask your soul to give you guidance and tell you what to do to be wealthy. As you make your attunement, your own thoughts and feelings say, "I am frightened that I will always be poor." This fear makes you desperate for money immediately. In your attunement the forces of your soul are pouring into you in ways that do not involve words. They are the communications of a soul. The only satisfactory word for such a communication is the word *energy*. Thus, the energy of your soul pours into you, urging you to feel that you have the unlimited creative forces of God within you to use to make money in the physical world. That is the guidance that your soul is trying to give you. But imagine that the fear in your personality mingles with your soul energies and the result is that you hear a "voice" telling you to steal money in order to become wealthy. You can say, "My soul is guiding me to steal." Without being aware of it, you have accepted distorted words created by your fear as "guidance" from your soul.

When you open yourself and expand your awareness through your attunement, your thoughts and feelings can come closer to the truth. However, your human thoughts and feelings do not always reflect truth. Therefore, it is wise to intelligently examine anything that you believe to be guidance. If your "guidance" expresses something that is critical, judgmental, selfish, or negative, you can assume that your own personality is involved, for the forces of your soul and of God would never urge you to be limited and narrow. If the guidance is filled with fear, it is a human creation. If it is kind, understanding, loving, and encouraging, there is a *possibility* that your thoughts and feelings are more aligned with the truth. However, you cannot be certain. You will need to continue to evaluate, assess, and test, using your intelligence and your experience of human life to try to decide what is an inner truth, and what is your own self-created thinking and feeling.

It is also important to be aware that your own *desires* can strongly affect your feeling of being guided. For example, if you believe that you have received guidance that is telling you to leave your work, obligations, and family to travel around to save the world with brilliant teaching, it is wise to look at this honestly, in light of knowledge about your personality. What are your desires? Do you have a desire to escape family responsibility? What are your fears that would cause you to believe that the people in the world need saving? You will need to be quite familiar with your mental and emotional patterns so that you can see clearly when your desires are creating distortions in spiritual guidance that you are receiving.

At times, when you are not clear about your own motives in striving for guidance, you might need to ask your friends and loved ones, "What do you see that I am doing here? What personality patterns and desires do you think I may be mixing in with my guidance?" All human beings tend to see life from their own personal viewpoint, which is strong and intense, and which is deeply influenced by their individual desires. If you have certain distortions in your views of life, usually you will not see them, yet other people may see them clearly. Therefore, as you work to receive spiritual guidance, it can be very beneficial to go to others and ask them to help you see your own desires, beliefs, and attitudes more clearly. Other people can help you discover and heal any distortions that might exist in your personality patterns.

SLEEP, DREAMS, AND SPIRITUAL GUIDANCE

As you prepare yourself for an experience of spiritual realities, another important area to look at is the relationship between your sleep state and spiritual guidance. Understanding this area can help you more fully use the beneficial influences that flow into you throughout your life.

Sleep provides one of the most important connections between human personalities and eternal souls. The link between the human and the divine is restimulated and reinvigorated during periods of sleep. Without the energy connections that are made in the sleep state, it would be impossible for human personalities to remain in physical bodies.

During the waking part of your day, your conscious awareness creates certain barriers to the inflowing of the energies of spiritual realities. These barriers are created by your human negativity—your negative thoughts, feelings, beliefs, and so forth. Thus, while you are awake, you have the power to create such rigidity and distortion within your personality that you can *temporarily* limit how deep the forces of your soul can penetrate into your human structure.

When you are sleeping and not dreaming—during the

blank period of sleep—your conscious thoughts and feelings, with any distortions that they may contain, are set aside. This opens the way for an intensifying of the forces of your soul that pour into you. Thus, this blank period of sleep has certain important benefits for you.

First, the blank sleep state creates an opportunity for spiritual energies to flow more fully into your physical body. During the day, when you are awake, it takes a conscious effort, and usually a great deal of time, for you to identify and release the mental and emotional distortions that temporarily block the spiritual energies from fully entering the cells of your body. However, when you are asleep, your personality distortions are put aside naturally. Thus, during the blank part of the sleep state, the healing, rejuvenating forces of life can more fully stimulate the cells of your physical body.

There is also a certain kind of *spiritual guidance* that you receive in the sleep state. While you are awake, in every moment there is a constant stream of eternal energies pouring into you, from your soul and from other souls who guide you. Those energies are intended to guide you toward a fuller expression of yourself, yet most of the time your conscious awareness is so preoccupied with your human life in the physical world that you do not notice those guiding energies. Each night, while you are in the blank sleep period, the spiritual energies coming into you are intensified, and your interfering human thoughts and feelings are not in the way. Therefore, the guidance penetrates more deeply into your personality matrix of energies. However, you are not aware of the guidance that you are receiving during the blank period of sleep.

After the blank period of sleep the "guidance energies" that you have unknowingly received begin to move toward your conscious awareness. This begins the process of dreaming. As you start dreaming, your conscious awareness returns and you become aware of your dream. The spiritual guidance that you received during the blank stage of sleep comes into your dream, but now the guidance is intermingling with your personality structure, which includes your thoughts, feelings, attitudes, beliefs, and various unconscious patterns. These personality energies have a certain power over the guidance energies that you have been fed during the blank sleep period, and at times the personality energies can distort the meaning of that guidance. Therefore, the dreaming experience becomes a kind of "human translation" of divine guidance.

This translation of spiritual guidance into a dream experience is unknowingly created by your personality. Thus, the relative clarity or distortion of your personality patterns will determine how much of the actual guidance manifests itself clearly and accurately in your dream. If your personality is essentially honest and loving, the dream can be quite inspiring and close to the truth of what your soul and other souls have attempted to communicate to you during the blank sleep period. On the other hand, if your personality is filled with unhealed negativity, the dream might be only a distant echo of what the souls intended for you to understand.

You can understand from this that dreams can be a rich source of guidance for those who have a dedication to truth, and the stamina, persistence, courage, and wisdom to live their waking lives honestly and lovingly. For those who do not apply themselves to growth in the waking period, and who allow their fears to accumulate without healing them, the dream state can become a morass of confusion.

INTUITION

Intuition is an elusive human capacity that is misunderstood by many people. To begin your understanding, you can consider intuition to be *an inner faculty that allows you to know more about life than you can consciously perceive in the physical world.* Your intuition is an important tool that enables you to expand your human experience beyond what you can learn directly from physical reality. Yet for the greatest growth, your intuition needs to be intelligently integrated with your experience of the physical world.

For example, imagine that you are standing in front of a brick wall. You become angry and you hit the wall with your fist. This creates an experience of physical pain that teaches you that it is not wise to hit brick walls. In the future, if you believe that your intuition is telling you to hit brick walls, you will have the experience to know that it is not wise to follow such an impulse, and that the impulse is not from your intuition.

Knowledge about life that is rooted in your day-to-day experience of your physical, "animal" nature can be considered to be *factual* knowledge. If you do not gain enough factual knowledge about the world, you will find it difficult to fulfill yourself in your physical life, no matter how much you develop your intuition.

Yet, with *only* factual knowledge, you will be limited in your experience of the world. You need your intuition to gain knowledge of aspects of life that are *not* rooted in physical reality. Your intuition can bring you an inner knowledge about aspects of life that do not appear on the surface of the physical world.

At the human level, intuition can bring you an inner perception of hidden thoughts and feelings that other people have, but that are not expressed in any tangible way. For example, you can intuitively feel that a friend is angry, even though there is no angry facial expression or behavior to indicate the anger.

Some people will have a certain intuitive sensing of events that are about to take place. Although such experiences involve the use of intuition to know what cannot be factually known from physical reality, these experiences still align with human realities at the *physical* level of life.

There is a larger kind of intuition that involves the perception of that which is not physical, that which is larger than the human. You could call this *spiritual intuition*. Spiritual intuition is what you will open and use in your attunement process to become more consciously aware of the eternal realities that constantly pour into you throughout your life. You have the capacity to draw upon your spiritual intuition during your attunement periods to actually feel the movement of your own soul within your conscious experience.

NEGATIVE ENERGIES

Some people fear that if they open themselves to spiritual energies, they risk being invaded by bad, or "evil," forces. Given the personal negativity that some people experience inside themselves, this is an understandable attitude. Because of the distortion of their own fear and negative feelings, they come to believe that "bad" realities exist in the physical world; therefore, they assume that there must be bad realities in the spiritual world.

If you have been sad and frightened for many years, and you have not addressed that negativity to heal it, when you begin to make an attunement to spiritual realities, your negative thoughts and feelings might be intensified as you create an open, receptive state of consciousness during your attunement period. At such a moment you might create a *feeling* of being threatened by negative forces and energies from beyond earth. What you must understand is that you are *creating* such a feeling.

Some people believe that they have directly experienced "evil" spirits. They do not believe that they are creating such experiences because the experiences seem to be so real. Yet the truth is: *All negativity is human-created. There are no evil forces in life. There are no bad energies from beyond earth.*

Some people, particularly those who have been influenced by human-created religions that teach that there is a

95

"devil," have come to believe that the existence of human pain and suffering proves that there are evil forces, or a devil, behind the negativity. If you have such beliefs, be very patient with them. Simply accept them for the time being, knowing that they are *temporary thoughts and feelings* that you have *created*. Such beliefs cannot harm you, even though you might find them frightening. If you calmly accept such confused beliefs, talk about them with people you trust, and learn to heal the fear that they cause, then eventually you can heal all distorted beliefs in "evil." You can free yourself from your self-created negativity, and you can begin to discover the truth of life, which is:

The spiritual forces of life are all-pervasive, and they are *always* creative and positive.

The clearest way to guide yourself toward this truth is to remind yourself each day that *all of life* is permeated by these spiritual forces that are *harmony, order, creativity*, and *love*— forces that you can understand as God. *There are no other energies in all of the spiritual realms*. The only negativity that exists lives *temporarily* in human thoughts, feelings, and actions. Thus, as you make your attunement, you can rest assured that there are no negative forces to influence you as you open, except negative human thoughts, feelings, and actions. And they can be healed.

If you are extremely sensitive, and you are near people who are filled with extremely strong negativity, such as anger or hate, you might feel their "energy" of negativity as a slight disturbed feeling within yourself. However, such energy cannot damage you. Nor can it cause you to be negative in yourself. If you are near such people and you also are filled with your own strong self-created negativity, there might be a slight intensifying of your own feelings of negativity from their negative human energies. But, as you heal your own negativity, you cease to be oversensitive to the energy of negative feelings that others might create.

As you work with your attunement process, remind yourself each day that *all human negativity is temporary*. It will always change. *The harmonious spiritual forces of life are permanent*. They never change. They are always perfection and magnificence.

If you find that you are *constantly* filled with fear and negativity, if you continually experience emotional pain and suffering without healing, or if you seem unable to release your belief in "bad" energies, then it is not wise to focus on attunement and the opening of your consciousness. It is wise to go to those who can help you heal your negativity at the human level. After you have done some healing, you might feel that you are ready to begin an attunement process.

On the other hand, if you feel that you are working honestly to heal your normal fears and doubts, and your personality is not seriously exaggerated in negative ways, then you can say to yourself, "There can be no bad influences in my opening through the process of attunement." You can begin the attunement process with confidence that it will eventually lead you to a marvelous experience of the beauty and goodness of the one true force—the force of God—that permeates all of life.

ATTUNEMENT AND PERFECTION

Many people have created feelings of negativity about themselves—they feel unworthy, or imperfect—and they have a belief that they must be perfect within themselves before they can have an experience of their soul. In yourself, you have a sense of what you would be like if you were a perfect personality, and at times you may condemn yourself if you fall short of your perfect vision. Yet in your work with your attunement process, it will be important to remind yourself:

"I do not need to be perfect to experience my soul. As I am working day by day to attain my ideal of perfection in my

human expression, I will remember that *while I am working on my personality patterns* **I can still experience my soul. I do not need to wait until I feel that I am perfect."**

Remind yourself that while you are working with your attunement process, if you condemn yourself for not being perfect, you will create a habit of feeling inadequate, and you will take that feeling into your attunement period. Then even when you begin to achieve an experience of your soul, you will tend to feel incomplete because of your feelings of inadequacy.

Instead of condemning yourself for falling short of your perfect vision, if you establish a habit of *rejoicing in yourself for trying*, then you will create strong feelings of appreciation for yourself, and you will take those feelings into your attunement period. Feelings of appreciation for yourself will help you make the inner opening that is necessary to experience your soul.

Each day of your life you have the choice of either condemning yourself for falling short of your perfect vision, which will create feelings of inadequacy and pain that can block your attunement, or of choosing to appreciate and love yourself in every way, which will open you to the beautiful experience of your soul that you are seeking in your attunement process. Remind yourself again and again that you do not need to be *perfect* to feel your soul. You need only to be as honest, patient, and loving with yourself as you can. Not only will that bring you a more joyful inner experience, but you will also find that it will open you more to others so that you will continue to grow in your relationships with the people in your life.

YOUR SELF-ASSESSMENT

As you work with the attunement process that will be explored in the following two chapters, you can bring about deeper experiences if you combine your attunement to spiritual realities with a process of personal growth in your daily human expression. That growth can bring about a vigorous, ongoing expansion within your human experience that will amplify what you gain from your attunement. You can use your attunement process to draw upon the spiritual energies of life; then the growth of your personality will enable you to express those energies more powerfully through your daily thoughts, feelings, and actions in the world. The personal growth can be achieved by learning to use a *self-assessment*.

Your self-assessment is simply a process of applying yourself daily to a deep study and understanding of your patterns of *thinking, feeling*, and *choosing*. Although the process is simple, if you use it with sensitivity and patience, you will find that it can lead to very powerful changes that will help you break through old limiting patterns so that you can free your full potential to accomplish what you desire in your day-to-day life.

Your self-assessment process can enable you to lovingly oversee and creatively orchestrate the complexities of your inner life. It can help you notice where you are limiting yourself by narrow choices so that you can make the changes that will free you from those limits. For example, imagine that you are a composer. You have a fondness for the note of C. You do not like the other notes of the scale, and you begin to feel that it is too complicated to use all of them. It is much easier to use your favorite note of C. Without noticing, you begin to focus so much on the note of C that you gradually eliminate all other notes from your composition. Soon, you are writing a symphony composed of a single note played over and over again. You have done this so gradually that you do not even notice how you have limited your composition.

In a similar way you can unintentionally and unknowingly develop a habit of concentrating only upon the patterns of thinking, feeling, and choosing that are most comfortable for you, such as the experience of self-indulgence in physical pleasure, avoidance of people who challenge you, and various other ways of taking the easy way out by trying to eliminate the complexities of your life. Your self-assessment can help you learn to use all of the available notes in creating your composition of human life. When you are willing to observe, learn about, and utilize the layer upon layer of complexity in your inner experience, you rise to a new level of mastery of your human expression. You can even become excited about the complexity of life, knowing that this complexity enables you to create more richness and beauty. The more notes you have available, the more potential you have for creating a brilliant symphony.

In working with your self-assessment, it is wise to always assume that you have within you a greater depth of potential than you realize. As was pointed out in earlier chapters, you are linked to the forces that have created life, and the more you trust that depth of inner creative power, the more you will stimulate your ability to use it.

To carry out your self-assessment, each day you can sit silently for five or ten minutes, apart from your attunement period, and:

> **Lovingly *observe* your daily experience in order to become aware of the *choices* that you have made that day.**

Observing the choices you have made opens the possibility of making *new choices*. If you notice that you are using very few notes in your composition, you are free to say, "My symphony is becoming very limited. That is not fulfilling for me, nor does it open my full potential. I need to make some changes in the way I am creating." Your observation of limiting habits of choosing gives you a base of knowledge from which to say, "I desire to go in a *new* direction. I wish to make changes in my life."

Thus, your self-assessment is carried out by simply *noticing what you have done with your choices*. Each day when you do your self-assessment, you can prompt a deep examination of your choices by asking yourself:

"1. **How have I been living today?**
2. **What have been the primary focal points of my thinking, feeling, and choosing?**
3. **To what have I given my precious time and energy?**"

Answering such questions will enable you to understand the life themes to which you have devoted most of your attention. For example, imagine that in your observation you notice that you have been strongly focused upon a deep resentment of someone in your life. As you become aware of that, you can say to yourself, "I now acknowledge that one strong theme of my life today has been resentment." Of course, you would not criticize or condemn yourself for that fear. You would simply say, "What will be the impact upon my life if I continue to *choose* resentment? What do I wish to do about my pattern of resentment?"

Your inner questioning needs to be done very lovingly, with a kindly attitude toward yourself, as though you are studying the personality patterns of a dear friend, and you wish to give wisdom to that friend. You do not wish to criticize or condemn your friend for any confused or frightened patterns that you discover.

You can carry out the deep questioning in many areas of your life. You can make a very systematic inventory—questioning yourself in all important areas, writing down the answers that you discover so that you may study them and decide what to do with the knowledge you gain from your loving questioning. You might have a category of questioning and assessment for your *thought* patterns, *emotional* patterns, *creativity, relationships, spiritual quest, wealth, occupation*, and other areas that are important to you. In your questioning you would try to lovingly notice how you have lived each area. What have been your primary *beliefs* and *commitments* in all of those areas? After you answer those questions, you can decide:

"What kinds of changes do I wish to make in the future, in alignment with my highest ideals, and in accordance with the deeper spiritual experience that I am gaining in my daily attunement period?"

With this kind of patient and loving assessment, you can come to know more clearly who *you* temporarily are, in terms of your human personality expression at any moment. Then you can decide if you wish to make changes and express *you* in a different way.

As you work with your self-assessment each day, remind yourself that you live in accordance with certain natural "rhythms" of your human expression that are associated with such factors as your psychological makeup, social training, and even certain rhythms in your physical body. Thus, your human expression is very complex. To keep this in mind, you can say to yourself, "Even when I am growing, when I am working intelligently and diligently, when I am loving, opening, and healing, at times it will be quite natural to have certain rhythms that swing from tightness to looseness, from heaviness to lightness, from sadness to joy."

There can also be events in your life in the *outer* world that will stimulate sadness, fear, or negativity. You can work with them and try to heal them. Yet they are not always the cause of your negative experience. In some periods you may be sailing smoothly through the events of your life, without any terrible challenges or disasters, and still begin to feel sadness, or a feeling of being lost, or a discouragement about life. In such a moment you would not need to rush to deeply analyze yourself and say, "What terrible fear has seized me now?" In such moments you might say, "It is simply part of the many rhythms in my life. It is one of the heavier cycles in my human moods. It could be caused by many things that will simply pass. They do not need a great deal of attention from me."

In other moments, as you monitor and assess your day-to-day experience, you might see patterns that *do* need your close attention. For example, if you say, "I see that every day I am creating a strong feeling that I am not a lovable person," then you would recognize that this is not a passing mood, nor a temporary low rhythm. This is a *habit* of thinking and feeling. If you desire to create joy and health in your life, you will need to give some attention to changing such a habit pattern. You can consciously work with your thoughts and feelings of being an unlovable person by using the suggestions given in Chapter Three.

When you work with your self-assessment, it will be important to remind yourself, as was stressed earlier, that your human personality expressions of thinking, feeling, and choosing are *temporary* ones. They are *flexible* and *changeable*. They are not the *truth* of your being, even though they are very important expressions while you are alive in human form.

The truth of you, as emphasized throughout this book, is the underlying eternal magnificence of your existence as a soul. However, some of your choices in your day-to-day life can *hide* the truth, creating temporary human negativity. Other choices can *reveal* the truth, bringing forth beauty, harmony, joy, and love into your day-to-day experience.

It is very important to constantly remind yourself that the factor determining whether your daily experience will be distorted or reflect the truth is the *choices* that you make, moment by moment, day by day, throughout your human lifetime. Your human experience grows out of a constant interplay between choices that you make about *everything* in life. Your daily choices establish the habit patterns of thinking, feeling, and choosing that *become* your life. Thus, if you consistently make selfish, fearful choices, you can create a life of narrowness, pain, and suffering. If your choices are made with kindness, sensitivity, and love, you can create a life of openness and freedom.

Your self-assessment gives you the awareness of the

choices that are *creating* your life, and the power to change those choices. If you are willing to make a gentle, intelligent, loving assessment of yourself and your daily human expression, *you will learn to recognize what choices you have made, and are making, that distort your human life*, that bring the pain and suffering that are so difficult to bear. *You will also learn to recognize the choices that you have made, and are making, that bring forth your underlying magnificence into your day-to-day experience.*

In the complex interaction of factors that create your human experience, there are many *hidden* patterns that you can understand as habits from your past lifetimes on earth. You, as a soul, have *intentionally* brought such past patterns into this lifetime as part of your present personality, for important reasons. Most of your past habit patterns are very creative and positive. They are your talents and abilities. Lesser numbers of them can be tendencies toward doubt or fear.

The presence of these past patterns can make your inner self-assessment a bit more complex. Since such patterns are usually hidden from your conscious awareness, they can be difficult to find. However, if you are patient, if you take a loving approach to your self-assessment, in time you may discover the patterns from the past that need your attention.

As you use your self-assessment to learn more about yourself, you can imagine that managing the numerous complicated threads of your human personality is like sailing a very large ship. There are many complexities involved in sailing such a ship—different sails to trim, ropes to manage, delicate equipment to use. Those complexities represent all of your shifting and changing human personality patterns of thinking, feeling, choosing, acting, believing, and so forth. Yet while you are sailing your ship of personality expression—adjusting all of your complexities—you are always moving in a direction toward your destination. The complexities of your life are interesting, and they are important to learn about and eventually master. But they do not change the fact that you are moving toward a destination of fullness and largeness in your human expression. Your destination as a human being is the blossoming of eternal qualities that you have brought into human life, time and time again, attempting to unfold and express them completely, and to link that expression with larger realities beyond the physical world.

All of your daily adjustments of personality complexities are important. But if, on a certain day, you would say, "I did not make a perfect adjustment," so be it. Remind yourself that your course is still steady. You are moving toward that fullness of expression in human form that is the purpose of your life on earth.

Keep in mind that in your self-assessment not only do you wish to identify areas of personal expression that you desire to change, but it is also important to *search for positive signs of achievement that you are making*. Many people have a tendency to focus too much upon the negative patterns within themselves. As you work with your self-assessment, be aware of any such tendencies and adjust for them by reminding yourself:

> **"In combining the spiritual experience from my attunement period with the personal growth of my self-assessment, I will look for *positive* indications within myself that I am deepening my life, that I am broadening and expanding my experience. I will look for ways in which I am bringing a greater understanding of my personality patterns into a fuller experience of my eternal nature."**

You can eventually establish a dedication to looking for *goodness* within yourself. That kind of positive assessment can convince you that, indeed, you are beginning to gain a mastery over your day-to-day human expression. You will then open your capacity to see quite clearly that within your human personality there shines forth the divine forces that have created all life.

BALANCING THE HUMAN AND THE DIVINE

As you master your life choices, you will come to understand that you can actually *choose* what kind of experience you desire to have. You will clearly realize that what you experience depends upon *what you choose to focus upon, moment by moment, each day of your life*. You can choose to focus upon your *human* experience of the moment, or you can choose to focus upon your *divine* nature as an eternal soul.

To choose a spiritual experience, you must consistently choose to bring the spiritual realities into the foreground of your awareness. Each day you must choose, again and again, to integrate a spiritual experience into your daily life, constantly returning to that choice in order to create the depth of experience that you desire.

If you choose to lose yourself completely in the physical world, your life will tend to be narrow and not totally fulfilling. If you choose to master the physical world while also opening yourself to a direct experience of spiritual realities, you can fulfill yourself in very deep ways.

By making your choices with wisdom and love each day, you will be able to balance the human and the divine in your life. From your own experience with your attunement process and your self-assessment, you will learn how much attention you need to put upon your physical life and how much upon your divine nature. You will establish a joyful interplay between your ordinary experience in the physical world and your expanded awareness of spiritual realities.

It is wise to think of the balance between your ordinary human experience and your experience of spiritual realities as a constantly changing situation that depends upon many factors in your day-to-day life—your mood, desires, interests, life circumstances, and so forth. Considering all of the complexities of each day, *you* will decide when you need to focus fully upon your human experience and when you wish to focus upon spiritual realities. You are the only one who can satisfactorily determine the perfect balance for you at any moment.

In working to establish this balance, it is wise to remind yourself that since you are a very complex being, it will not always be a simple matter to harmonize the many aspects of your human nature with your eternal existence. While you are living in your physical body, you will naturally have strong desires for your own personal fulfillment in the physical world. There is a natural "animal" tendency toward selfishness and self-involvement with physical pleasures. To help balance this tendency, you can remind yourself that if you put all of your attention upon self-involvement, you might eventually become uncaring, unfeeling, and insensitive to other people. Such a focus would bring pain and suffering, and it would temporarily cover over your deep intuitive abilities to experience spiritual realities.

On the other hand, if you totally ignore your personal fulfillment, you can begin to feel empty and frustrated in your daily life. You might begin to feel that there is no purpose for your human expression. If you create a deep spiritual experience under such conditions, you might tend to use your spiritual pathway in a distorted way as an escape from the feelings of incompleteness that you have in your physical life.

As you work with your attunement process and your self-assessment day by day, you will tend to fluctuate back and forth between a focus upon your human fulfillment and your experience of spiritual realities. But there will usually be a need to give a certain priority to your humanness, especially when it makes strong demands upon you. For example, if you are struggling desperately to make money to support a family, you may not be so interested in having a spiritual experience. For a while your attention will need to be focused primarily upon satisfying your human needs in the physical world.

You can consider that, temporarily, you owe a certain allegiance to your physical body and to your "animal" nature. However, you must decide *how much* attention to give to your important human expression. Will you simply sustain your body at a minimal level by just feeding and clothing it, or will you give a lot of attention to the sensual pleasures of the body? You are the one who must decide what the perfect balance will be each day. And what you believe to be the perfect balance can change. For example, if you have not had sexual fulfillment for many months, then your sexual desires might become very important, and you may give them a great deal of attention for a while. On the other hand, if you have continually indulged in sexual fulfillment for a long period, then it may not be so important, and you will turn your attention elsewhere.

You can achieve your optimum balance each day by using your self-assessment process to alertly and honestly monitor your thoughts, feelings, desires, choices, and actions. Then you can learn to patiently and lovingly adjust your various patterns in relationship to the people around you, so that you can bring about the balance between the human and the divine that serves you best each day of your life.

The knowledge in this chapter is an important foundation for your inner work. As you integrate these insights into your thinking and feeling, you will find that you can create a sense of confidence in your ability to make an inner opening. With that confidence you are then ready to turn your attention to the first stage of the actual attunement process that will lead you to a direct experience of your soul.

CHAPTER FIVE

Your Beginning Attunement

———— ✳ ————

It is wise to approach your attunement to your soul in two stages. In this chapter you will explore the first stage—the beginning experience of attunement. This initial preparation will help you create a refined level of sensitivity that will enable you to then move on to the second stage—the deeper attunement process that will be explored in the next chapter.

To feel how these two stages are related, imagine that you are searching for the doorway to a beautiful room in a house that has two stories. You are looking for the doorway on the first floor, but the room that you desire to find is on the second floor of the house. No matter how hard you look on the first floor, you will never find the doorway on the second floor. But if you are willing to walk up the stairs, it will not take much searching to find that doorway.

A profound experience of your soul is the room on the second floor. It is a "higher" accomplishment than your normal experience, which, you might say, exists on the "first floor" of consciousness. Walking up the stairs represents the practice that you will do with a beginning attunement process. This practice will help you learn how to make the inner opening that will enable you to eventually have the profound spiritual experience you desire.

In moving toward a deep experience of your soul, if you do the preliminary work of making the simpler attunement, then it will not be so difficult later to do the deep attunement process that will lead you to your soul. If you are willing to walk up the stairs to the second floor, it will not be so difficult to find the doorway there.

CONSISTENCY IN YOUR ATTUNEMENT

It is very important to practice your attunement process consistently, day after day. Because of the intensity of your experience of physical reality, and because you give so much of your attention to the affairs of your daily life, the physical world naturally holds a considerable power over your human consciousness. If you do not consistently set aside some time each day to temporarily disengage from your fascination with the physical world, and open yourself to a larger reality, you can often feel helpless in the face of a seemingly overwhelming physical reality that at times appears to press upon you from all sides, allowing no possible escape. In order to build up a strong inner spiritual life that can stand up against this influence of the physical world, you need a day-to-day consistency in your attunement process.

Each day, as you do your attunement, you are *choosing* to open yourself to spiritual realities. If you make that choice consistently and persistently, your experience in the attunement process can grow and grow. Your awareness of the magnificence of life can steadily expand as a result of practicing your attunement each day.

You cannot expect to achieve a deep spiritual experience in a short period. However, when you make a deep commitment to yourself to do your attunement each day, you set out upon a pathway that will eventually bring forth an *inner power* that you can use to balance the strong outer influences of the physical world.

As your attunement experience becomes more satisfying and inspiring, you will find that eventually you will never tire of seeking a deeper and deeper experience of the beauty and love of the spiritual realities. You will approach your attunement period as something to which you gladly return again and again, knowing that the more you enter your deep attunement, the more it will enrich your life.

Once you become consistent in your attunement, then each day after your attunement period you can return to your daily life in the physical world with a deeper sensitivity to the way that the spiritual forces permeate your ordinary human experience. You can eventually choose to be constantly open to a spiritual experience throughout the day. Thus, your consistency in your attunement process will contribute to a deep spiritual feeling about all of life.

RUSHING TOWARD THE FUTURE

One pattern that is important to monitor as you make your attunement is the human tendency to ignore the present moment and rush toward the future. When you feel incomplete in the present, you might begin to imagine some kind of fulfillment that you can achieve in the future. Then you try to do everything you can to rush toward that future fulfillment so that you can feel satisfied and complete. The result is that you lose touch with the present moment, and you miss out on what is contained in that moment.

When you sit in the silence of your attunement moment, you might at times feel incomplete, or unsatisfied with your attunement experience in that moment. You might stir up a strong desire to move toward a deeper experience of your soul in order to feel complete or more satisfied. Since you are not having such an experience in the present moment, you automatically try to move forward to a *future* moment in which you will have the deep experience of your soul that you desire. This causes you to step out of the present moment and miss the energies of your soul that are flowing into you in that moment.

In your attunement period, when you feel the impulse to rush toward the future, notice that impulse, then release it. Avoid the temptation to strive to move forward. Say to yourself:

"In this very moment, the beauty and the love of my soul are pouring into me. I now release myself into *this* moment so that I may receive these beautiful gifts from my soul."

LEARNING TO ATTUNE TO YOUR SOUL

Mastering a beginning attunement—walking up the stairs to the second floor—involves, first, learning to make *a deep relaxation of your physical body*. Then you will learn to *calm your thoughts and feelings that have to do with the physical world*, or they will tend to overpower moments of silence in which you are attempting to make an attunement to your soul.

Next, you will develop the ability to *project yourself in your imagination beyond your present limited experience of yourself as a human being*. Your experience as a human being is intentionally limited by your soul in order to allow you to have an extremely intense experience of your human Self in this lifetime. If your human experience was not limited, your consciousness would wander off into areas so large that it would be difficult for you to remain *yourself* as a present individual human being. You would wander beyond yourself. You would lose your sense of Self in its association with your present personality and body.

If, through your own choice, you decide, "I wish to experience my soul, I wish to consciously experience eternal realities," then it is a bit like swimming upstream. In your ordinary life it is as if you have jumped into a river intending to float *down*stream. In other words, you have come into human form intending to experience yourself as one human being, without the eternal realities impinging upon your human consciousness and distracting you. However, you are free to say, "For a while I wish to swim upstream." You are free to expand your normal awareness to include a perception of spiritual realities. But you must realize that it will take some effort to swim upstream. It will not come naturally like floating downstream. It is "natural" for you to float downstream, to simply be yourself in the ordinary human way. But it requires strength and stamina to swim upstream, to turn your awareness away from the physical world in order to gain a clear perception of *non*physical realities. When you wish to consciously experience your soul, it requires a strong inner ability to lift yourself out of your ordinary human experience.

You can set the stage for this accomplishment by using the following beginning attunement process of seven steps. You may desire to learn one step at a time before you go on to the next step. If you do this, make certain to always do Step Seven, returning to your normal awareness, at the end of each attunement period. If you feel confident in your inner abilities, you may wish to begin by practicing all seven steps at the same time.

STEP ONE: RETREATING FROM THE WORLD

To begin your attunement process, select a quiet, restful place of privacy to which you can retreat each day. This is where you will withdraw from the intensity and drama of your daily life so that you can learn to release the powerful distractions of the physical world. Each day:

Seek out a place of beauty and peacefulness where you will have complete privacy for your entire attunement period. If you can retreat to this same place each day, you will find that you develop a comfortable, secure feeling about your private attunement sanctuary. It will be easier to

feel untroubled by the cares and responsibilities of your daily life.

STEP TWO: RELAXING YOUR BODY

Most people are filled with tension from the stress and strain of their daily pursuits in the physical world. This tension affects your body and mind, making it difficult for you to attain the physical relaxation that is necessary to release yourself into a deep attunement. The habit of holding your body tense and stiff engages your brain in a way that can keep your mind agitated. This makes it difficult to calm your mind so that you can use it to expand your awareness in the attunement process. Therefore, the goal of this step of your attunement process is *relaxation of your physical body*.

Although the relaxation of your body might seem like a simple task to accomplish, many people find that when they begin the attunement process they discover that the habit of holding their body stiff is much stronger than they realized. They find that they have difficulty actually letting go of the tension in their body. Therefore, you may need to work patiently with this step.

Begin this step of your attunement process in this way:

Sit comfortably with your body in a position that you can hold without any strain. Experiment until you find the most comfortable position. You might wish to avoid lying down, since you are more likely to fall asleep in that position.

After you are comfortable, close your eyes. Take a few deep breaths. Then begin to relax your body. Silently speak relaxing words to yourself. Your body will follow your silent command to release tension. You can say to yourself: "In this moment I let go of all tension in my body. My body is now relaxing. It is becoming very loose and flexible. All effort is now being released. My body is relaxing deeply now. It is

entering such a deep, calm state of relaxation that I feel wonderfully restful and content." Do this for as long as you desire.

Next, turn your attention, in a slow, gentle way, to your breathing. Simply notice your breathing, not trying to do anything special with it. Gently become aware of your breathing, and continue to relax.

If you are not used to sitting still and relaxing, this first step of your attunement process might be surprisingly difficult. Simply do it each day, without any concern. Make it pleasant and enjoyable, avoiding the temptation to try to rush into a future moment when you believe you will have a deeper experience. Remember that the beautiful forces of your soul are pouring into you even when you are simply sitting and relaxing, doing nothing.

Work with this first step of the attunement process until you can easily slip into a deep relaxation. For a while you may spend your attunement period each day simply sitting and relaxing. Make sure that you can completely relax yourself before you add the second step of the attunement process; otherwise, the tension in your body will distract you from deepening your attunement experience.

If it is easy for you to relax your physical body, you might master this step of the attunement process quite quickly. Then add the next step of the process.

After your attunement period each day, remember to do Step Seven, the return to normal awareness.

STEP THREE: RELEASING YOUR THOUGHTS AND EMOTIONS

The next step in your attunement process is learning to create an inner release from your strong attachment to your normal thoughts and emotions that are rooted in physical reality. The primary task will be to disengage from your continual stream of thinking about your daily life.

Thinking is obviously a valuable activity in your ordinary life. However, it is a *human* activity. Your thoughts can be beautiful, please you, and serve you in the physical world. But during your attunement period, if you remain focused on human-created thoughts, you will not be able to move toward *divine experience*. You will simply be swept downstream in your normal human experience.

However, since your ordinary awareness is continually overshadowed by your thinking, you might find that during the initial stages of your attunement work your everyday thoughts and emotions seem to be dominating your inner experience. You might find that you are thinking about your work, your debts, what you want to buy, a trip that you want to take—the strong concerns that relate to your existence in the physical world. Thus, for many people, their first attempts at this step of the attunement process may be frustrating or discouraging. It will require patience and persistence on your part to continue to pursue your attunement process with optimism, and with the confidence that you will eventually learn how to release those thoughts and emotions that tie you to the physical world so that you can make the breakthrough to deeper realities.

Many people who try to have a spiritual experience believe that in order to be successful they must have a period of absolute inner silence in which they cease *all* thinking. This can be a very difficult task to accomplish. Your thoughts are strong and persistent. If you set your goal as the suppression of all thoughts, you can inadvertently establish an inner tension because you are working against the natural tendency of your human mind to continually create thoughts.

A more productive approach is to learn to simply *ignore* your thoughts while they are happening. You can let them come forth in their natural way, but you do not need to pay attention to them or become caught up in them. With practice, you can learn to direct your inner awareness *away* from your thoughts while they are continuing within you. In a sense you learn to *feel beyond your thoughts*, with a kind of *inner sensing*. This will enable you to relax so that you will not generate the inner tension that comes from trying to completely suppress your thoughts.

Each day, after you have done the previous steps of your attunement process, practice accomplishing this:

> **As you sit in the silence, in a calm, patient way, allow your ordinary thoughts and emotions to simply drift away, instead of trying to eliminate them. Let your attention wander into an "area above" your thoughts and emotions, as though your attention is gently and effortlessly floating away. You can feel that your thoughts and emotions are heavy energies that are sinking down and slipping out of your awareness, while your awareness is a joyful inner field of focus that is light and airy, slowly and softly lifting up. You are riding that light, airy awareness as it gradually floats upward, away from your heavier thoughts and emotions.**

In time you will become adept at simply ignoring whatever thoughts and emotions might arise during this step of your attunement process. You will be able to gently release your attention from your process of thinking and generating emotions.

As you learn to turn your awareness away in this manner, you will find that you eventually feel as if you are slipping away from your thoughts and emotions. Either they will seem to fade into the background of your awareness or they will cease for a while. Either way you will not notice what is happening because you will not be paying attention to your thoughts and emotions. You will not be concerned with what they are doing. Your awareness will be floating away in a beautiful release from the physical world.

In this step of your attunement process you are essentially learning to pause in midstream in the flow of ordinary human thinking and feeling that usually carries you downstream into normal experience. You are learning to stay poised in that stream so that you will not be carried away by it.

STEP FOUR: PROJECTING BEYOND THE HUMAN

The next step is to use your *imagination* to project yourself beyond your human experience in the physical world. You can accomplish this in the following manner:

> **Begin to imagine yourself floating upward, out of your ordinary experience. You are leaving behind the physical earth and your ordinary human perceptions. Imagine that you are now turning toward a new experience of freedom. Imagine that you are preparing to move toward your soul.**
>
> **Next, begin to imagine that you are a nonphysical being floating freely above the physical earth. You are floating in a marvelous existence of *love*.**

You can imagine many things to help project yourself beyond the ordinary human experience. By using your imagination in this way, you create certain inner experiences that are different from your ordinary perceptions, that lift you up out of the normal flow of experience in which you are usually caught.

In the previous step you were learning to pause in the downstream current of human experience. In this step you can imagine that you are now turning against that current. This is the first step in preparing to swim upstream—gaining enough energy or force against the ordinary current of human consciousness to simply turn against that current and hold yourself in place, mentally speaking. By turning against the onrushing current of ordinary experience, you are preparing yourself for a strong movement upstream.

This step need not be difficult, although you can make it

difficult if you are not confident in your abilities and continually doubt yourself. If you simply do this step each day in a calm, confident way, expecting to be successful at it, then this step of your attunement process can be quite relaxing and freeing, mentally and emotionally.

STEP FIVE: GAINING INTENSITY AND DEPTH

The next step in your attunement process is to gain some thrust against the current of ordinary experience so that you can begin to move upstream. You will gain intensity and depth in your inner experience so that you can move in a different direction in your awareness, away from the ordinary human experience, toward an experience of yourself as an eternal soul.

This is where you will begin to use your *will* to thrust forward against the stream of ordinary awareness. You can consider that you will be using your will to gain an elevation of your consciousness *beyond* imagination.

At first this might be difficult for you. It is not so difficult to imagine leaving your body, or to imagine being a soul existing in a spiritual realm. You can imagine many things. However, when it is time to imagine something *beyond* your imagination, it can be a bit confusing.

In this step of moving further beyond human awareness in its ordinary sense, you need to learn to make the difficult movement of imagining what you cannot imagine. You can accomplish this by using your will to create a *feeling*. In the previous step you imagined yourself existing as a nonphysical being floating above the earth in a realm of love. In this step:

Begin to imagine that as you float in a beautiful realm of love, you are now *becoming the love*. Use your will to give yourself to a free-floating experience in which, even though you

may not know exactly how to imagine becoming love, you do it nonetheless. Using your will, set your intention to become the love that you have imagined.

After you set your intention, release. Simply become the feeling of love.

As you practice this step of the attunement process each day, you will discover that you have an inner knack for entering a feeling that goes beyond what you can actually imagine. You will learn to enter an inner experience that cannot be clearly defined by your mind, but it can be deeply felt in a way that will enable you to make a strong inner opening within yourself.

STEP SIX: RELEASING INTO YOUR SOUL

The next step in your attunement process is to realize that in the stream of experience that ordinarily sweeps you downstream into the normal human experience, there is a hidden second current that moves *upstream*. Once you have learned the previous steps, you will find that if you are able to release your will at this point in the attunement process, you will discover a new *inner momentum*. This is the movement of your soul, which can begin to carry you away from ordinary human awareness toward a deeper experience of reality. It can happen without any willing or effort on your part.

This second current in your stream of inner experience is a very subtle one, and at first it may not be apparent. Therefore, it will take patience and persistence with this step of the attunement process in order to be successful.

Each day, after you have completed the previous steps of the attunement process, and are successfully imagining yourself as the feeling of love:

Begin to give up all willing and striving. Give up all desire to *do*. Release yourself into simply *being*. Become the

experience of the moment, without exerting any personal influence over the moment or trying to control it. Become softness and *receptivity*, without striving. Simply release yourself into a gentle current that will carry you toward your soul. Release completely and allow your soul to carry you toward the experience you need in the moment.

Do this step for as long as you desire. When you feel that you have completed the experience to your satisfaction for that day, then turn your attention to Step Seven, your return to normal awareness.

STEP SEVEN: RETURNING TO NORMAL AWARENESS

After each attunement period, always bring yourself back to your ordinary awareness in a slow, unhurried manner. Each day you can return to your normal awareness in this way:

Begin to slowly let go of the expanded awareness that you attained during your attunement period. Let the experience of expansion begin to drift away. Create a feeling of gently moving back toward your ordinary experience of yourself. Do this quite slowly, taking as much time as you need to return to your normal awareness.

Next, turn your attention to your physical body. Notice how your body feels. Pay attention to any physical sensations that you are experiencing.

Then begin to pay attention to the room about you. Notice what the air feels like. Listen for sounds in the outer world.

Next, begin to think about your daily affairs and what you will do in the physical world. Create a feeling of eagerness to take up the activities of your daily life with a new sense of inspiration and rejuvenation.

When you feel completely ready, slowly open your eyes. Sit for a moment or two so that you can regain your equilib-

rium, then slowly rise and joyfully resume your activities in the physical world.

These are steps for the first stage of an attunement process that you can eventually refine and deepen. They will give you the experience with the inner adjustment of your thoughts, feelings, and willing that is necessary to prepare you for a deeper penetration into spiritual realities. This first stage of the attunement process can eventually become the stable platform upon which you build a profound experience of your soul.

CHAPTER SIX

A Deeper Experience
of Your Soul

------------ ✳ ------------

If you have practiced the beginning attunement consistently and patiently, you should now feel prepared to learn how to make a deeper attunement to your soul and to the spiritual realities of life. In this chapter you will find specific ways to work with your awareness in order to master a deeper attunement process.

As you work with this deep attunement process, remind yourself that because you are used to the intensity and dramatic nature of your human perceptions of physical reality, you might expect this deep attunement to yield experiences of spiritual realities that are as *intense* as your experiences in the physical world. You might expect your perceptions of spiritual realities to be as strong and impactful as those of physical realities. This is not likely to be the case.

If you were to *constantly* enter into a strong, dramatic experience of spiritual realities while living on earth, you would be so overpowered by that experience that all else in your human life would pale by comparison. You would be so overwhelmed by the intensity of the spiritual realities that nothing else in life would seem worth your attention. You would have only one choice in life that would seem worth making—to focus upon spiritual realities. That would essentially rob you of your free will, your right to choose in human life.

During your deep attunement period your soul will not usually overpower your human experience. The forces of your soul, and of God, will not usually appear to you so strongly that they blot out all of your ordinary awareness. You will be left free to *choose* where to focus your attention in each moment.

Therefore, as you use the following deep attunement process, it should not be surprising to you if your initial perceptions of deeper spiritual realities are relatively dim. At first you might simply notice some subtle feelings of peace, harmony, or love. Some people might have a vague sense of an inner *movement* that is felt to be comforting and soothing. From such early experiences you can expect your perceptions of spiritual realities to grow in a gradual way. This gradual unfoldment of your spiritual perceptions allows you to slowly and gently open to the spiritual realities, while you continue to appreciate and value your day-to-day experience in the physical world.

WORKING WITH THE DEEP ATTUNEMENT PROCESS

As you look at the following steps of the deep attunement process, you will notice that subtle inner adjustments are involved in some of the steps. It might take some time to learn to make those adjustments. Therefore, in using this attunement process, you will find it helpful to work with it in stages. You can think of yourself as a brilliant dancer who must learn an intricate new dance. First of all you remind yourself that you are a master of dance, and you remember that your abilities are very strong. Then you decide that you do not need to learn the entire dance all at once. You will learn it one step at a time.

You will begin with the first step of the dance, and you will practice it until you know it. Then you will add the next step, and you will do the first and second steps together for a while until you can do them both. Next, you will add the third step of the dance, and you will practice all three steps together until you master them. You will continue adding one step at a time in this way until, finally, you have put the many individual steps together in a beautiful sequence that becomes the complete dance.

Even though the dance might be difficult to learn, once you master it you feel a profound sense of accomplishment and joy. And you realize that you have been expanded and made larger by the work that you have done. You are now a more evolved master of the dance.

So it is with your daily work with this deep attunement process. You can begin your work with the attitude that you are a master of human life. You have lived many lifetimes through a long period on earth, even though you may not be aware of that past experience. You have very strong talents and abilities that you have developed through those many lifetimes, and you will bring them to bear upon the new dance—the experience of opening your present human personality to an expanded awareness of its eternal soul. Approaching your deep attunement with a feeling of confidence and trust in your ability to succeed will stimulate your mental and emotional energies in a way that will help you successfully make the attunement.

You will then work with the following deep attunement process, one step at a time, with one exception. You will notice that the deep attunement process consists of seven steps. As with the beginning attunement process, Step Seven is a gradual return to normal awareness. Step Seven should be done at the end of *every* attunement period.

Therefore, begin your advanced attunement work by confidently addressing the first step of the attunement process and practicing it day after day until you feel that you are beginning to master it. Each day, after you have done Step One for as long as you desire, end your attunement period by doing Step Seven of the process, the return to normal awareness.

Next, add the second step, and practice Steps One and

Two together, ending every attunement period with Step
Seven. Then add Step Three of the sequence, and do Steps
One, Two, and Three, ending with Step Seven. Continue to
add a new step as you master the previous ones, until all of
the steps flow together in a beautiful movement each time
you do your attunement.

As you set out to do the deep attunement process that will
now be described, it is wise to begin by reading the entire
chapter so that you will be familiar with the whole attunement sequence. When you are ready to begin your actual
attunement, return to the first step, read the description, try
to deeply understand and *feel* the suggestions for accomplishing Step One, then sit in silence and put the suggestions
into practice.

STEP ONE: BEGINNING YOUR DEEP ATTUNEMENT

Begin your deep attunement period in the same way that
you began the simple attunement suggested in the last chapter. Go to your private place and enter a silence. Release the
distractions of your daily human life. Release all physical
tension. Relax your physical body.

Just as you did with the simple attunement process:

> **Sit comfortably with your eyes closed. Take a few deep
> breaths. Continue to relax your body. Silently speak relaxing
> words to yourself. Say to yourself inwardly: "In this moment
> I release all tension in my thoughts, emotions, and body. My
> body is now relaxing more and more. I am now entering a
> deep, calm state of relaxation. I feel completely relaxed and
> very peaceful." Do this for as long as you desire.**
>
> **Next, notice your breathing. Without any effort, simply
> become aware of your breathing. Do not try to adjust your
> breathing or control it. Simply notice it, and continue to
> relax.**

After you have done this step of the deep attunement process, if you feel accomplished at relaxing, go on to the second step. If you still find it difficult to relax, do Step One for as long as you wish, then go on to Step Seven, the gentle return to normal awareness.

STEP TWO: RELEASING PHYSICAL REALITY

The next step in the deep attunement process is also similar to the earlier simple attunement, but it combines the earlier release of thoughts and feelings with a release of the physical world. You will begin by creating your inner release from your normal thoughts and feelings. Begin to disengage from thinking about your daily life within physical reality.

Remember that your thoughts can be strong and persistent. You are not attempting to eliminate your thoughts. You simply wish to ignore them. You do not need to pay attention to or become caught up in them.

In this step of your deep attunement:

> **Direct your inner awareness away from your thoughts. Use your inner sensing to feel beyond your thoughts. Allow your thoughts to drift away. Let your attention wander beyond your thoughts. Let your attention gently float away from your thoughts. Allow your awareness to drift gently upward, above your thoughts.**
>
> **Then imagine that you are beginning to drift away from the physical world. You are beginning to slowly float upward above the earth. You are feeling yourself leaving behind all heaviness, all burdens. You are floating away from all physical reality.**

After you have done this step of your attunement, if you feel ready, go on to Step Three. If you feel you need more practice with releasing the physical reality, do this step for as long as you desire, then do Step Seven, the return to normal awareness.

STEP THREE: CREATING HARMONY AND LOVE

When you feel that you can comfortably put aside the physical world, the next step to add to your deep attunement process is a focus upon your *inner landscape*, where you will create feelings of harmony and love. Such feelings are an important factor in your movement toward an experience of your soul.

During this period of your attunement you will continue to release any thoughts that might arise. You do not wish to limit yourself to thinking. You will learn to go beyond your thoughts. You can say to yourself, "If thinking is a human-created activity, when I turn to my inner landscape and attempt to grasp it by thinking alone, I am limiting myself. I am trying to chop down a forest with a small carving knife." You have other, more powerful implements available to you, such as your imagination, intuition, will, and other creative forces.

Of course, your thoughts of the physical world can be persistent, and even though you may have succeeded in ignoring them in the previous step of this attunement process, they may be stirred up again during this step. At this point simply *accept* random thoughts, without letting them interfere with the beauty that you will be creating in your inner landscape. This would be similar to coming into a beautiful field of flowers, and as you look about the field you notice a few weeds here and there. You are free to ignore the many colorful flowers, focus on the few weeds, and say, "What a terrible field. It is filled with weeds." You are also free to notice the weeds, accept them as part of the field, and then turn your attention to the beauty of the flowers. You realize that the weeds may not please you, but they do not destroy the beauty of the flowers.

In a similar way, as you enter your inner landscape of harmony and love, notice any weeds of random thoughts. Accept them, without feeling that they are ruining your attunement. Know that a few thoughts will not diminish the beauty of the inner experience that you are about to create. Accept the thoughts for a moment, then use your imagination to begin to wander away from them.

At this point it is important to understand the difference between *thinking* and *paying attention*. Even while your mind is *thinking* about something else, you can learn to *pay attention* to your inner landscape of harmony and love. Your attention can begin to enter into your inner landscape with your awareness.

Each day, after you have done Steps One and Two of your deep attunement process, begin to create your inner landscape of harmony and love by accomplishing this:

> **Accepting and ignoring any thoughts that might arise, gently use your will to pay attention to your imagination. Direct your imagination to align with your intuitive capacity in order to begin the creation of your inner landscape of harmony and love. Initiate this by imagining a *setting* that inspires in you feelings of harmony and love. You might imagine a beautiful place in nature or a place of holiness. This might mean that you begin to sense a setting from a past lifetime, such as a temple in Greece, a holy shrine in ancient China, or a sacred initiation chamber in ancient Egypt.**
>
> **As you begin this imagining, invite feelings of harmony and love into your heart. Also, imagine that the powerful intuitive capacity that lives within you is coming forward into the moment. Inwardly feel that you are intuitively aligning with a deep inner wisdom within you. That wisdom is helping you create feelings of harmony and love. Feel that this inner wisdom is also helping you create the beautiful vision of your inner landscape.**

If at first your mind finds this activity to be rather vague, simply ignore such thoughts and *do* this step. Try to *feel* this activity, and do it inwardly to the best of your ability, without thinking about it. You do not need to pay attention to any demands that your mind might make to *know* what you are doing. You can learn to create an inner landscape of harmony and love in an intuitive way, without knowing in your mind exactly what you are doing. You do not need to know *how* to do this. Simply do it in any way that you can. In time your intuitive knowing will guide you, and this step of the attunement process will lead you to an inner experience that is quite inspiring.

> **Next, use your imagination to place yourself fully into the inner landscape that you have created. Enter that landscape and begin to live within it with great abandonment and joy.**

This can be a very delicate maneuver. Most people, in attempting to imaginatively enter their inner landscape, will tend to use a vision of their present personality, which can have within it human pain, suffering, and feelings of limit. Instead of taking into your inner landscape any temporary human illusion of negativity, you wish to color your inner landscape with *truth*. Therefore, when you imaginatively insert yourself into your inner landscape, do not take with you the temporary challenges, fears, or human distortions of your daily life. Those are not the truth of your being. Use your imagination to see yourself in your inner landscape as a magnificent being who has wonderful, unlimited qualities and abilities.

To feel how to make this inner shift, imagine that you have been invited to a grand palace. You know that the only guests invited are kings, queens, and other royalty from many countries. You believe that you are a peasant. Therefore, you assume that you have been invited to the palace to be a servant. You come to the back door of the palace and say, "Do you wish me to sweep? Do you wish me to collect the garbage?" Then you are told, "We expected you at the front door because you are the guest of honor." You suddenly realize that you have become confused about who you truly are.

This can give you a sense of what you will try to feel about yourself as you imagine yourself entering your inner landscape of harmony and love. You are not an insignificant, unworthy person coming to beg at the grand hall of spiritual realities. You are a soul of brilliance who has a place of honor in the palace of eternal existence.

It will take a certain inner flexibility to make this kind of adjustment. You will learn to put aside any rigid, limited beliefs that you might have about your worthiness by reminding yourself that you have positive inner qualities and abilities of which you are not fully aware. In the drama of your earth life, you have often forgotten your true Self and your greater abilities, believing that you are a peasant, when, in truth, you are nobility. You will now create new beliefs about your worthiness.

> **Next, turn your attention to the force that unites all beings in all realms of existence—the force of *love*. Be aware that a divine *energy* of love permeates all of life, and there is also the human *feeling* of love. Use your imagination and creativity to try to bring them both together in the beautiful inner landscape that you have created.**

Love is the unifying energy of all realms, so no matter where you exist, whether in physical form or in spiritual realities, there is always the energy of love. Thus, when you enter your inner landscape and align with *feelings* of love, you are beginning to align with the love *energies* that unite all realms of consciousness. You will eventually learn to ride the feelings of love into an awareness of the larger reality of love energies.

> **Next, in your inner landscape, as you attune to this love, begin to imagine that you are surrounded by loving souls who share the wonder of existence with you. Feel surrounded by beloved ones of an exalted nature. Feel joined to them by the energy of the love.**

This is a beginning stage of aligning with loving souls. Savor this experience. Indulge in it for a while. But know that, eventually, an inner wisdom in you will gradually lead you to more and more refined perceptions of these souls, and, consequently, of your own soul.

This is a way to create an inner landscape of love and harmony that is not overshadowed by human narrowness. When this process is used in conjunction with the patient, honest, loving self-assessment of your personality that was described earlier, you will feel that you are blossoming in many ways. The creative work that you do in your daily life with your personality will stimulate greater feelings of harmony and love that you can then bring into your attunement period. The inner work with your attunement will create harmony and love that you can take back into your daily life. When these two aspects of you are interacting in this way, you will experience a satisfying sense of wholeness and greater aliveness.

Do this step of your deep attunement, along with the first two steps, until you feel that you are comfortably experiencing harmony and love in your inner landscape. This does not mean that you will have a perfect experience every day. The depth of your experience can fluctuate, depending upon many factors in your daily life. Also, remember that your experience of the spiritual realms can be quite subtle and vague. You may not have experiences that are as tangible or dramatic as you might like. Yet if you are consistently having some feelings of harmony and love during this step of your attunement most of the time, then you can feel confident that you can add the next step to your attunement process.

Each day, after you have experienced this step of your deep attunement process for as long as you desire, end your attunement period with Step Seven, your return to normal awareness.

STEP FOUR: SETTING YOUR DIRECTION

After you have established harmony and love within your inner landscape, it is time to use your will to set the direction for your deep attunement. In this step you will decide what you wish to accomplish in your deep attunement experience. You will try to sense, or feel, what you wish to move toward. You will inwardly define where you wish to go with your deep attunement. This can be a loose and flexible sense of direction.

It is wise to begin with a feeling that you are intending to move toward an ideal that is quite noble. Setting your intention is a matter of making a *human* statement from within your personality, but that statement should reflect the beauty and nobility of the *eternal* realities toward which you desire to move. A noble, exalted intention makes it easier in your attunement period to match the energies of the spiritual realities with your own mental and emotional energies.

In setting your intention you might decide that you wish to move toward an experience of your own soul, or of souls who guide you, or of God itself. For most people, moving toward their own soul is usually a beneficial focus in the beginning stages of the deep attunement process.

If you establish an intention to move toward an experience of your soul, it will be natural to begin to wonder about the nature of your soul and to try to picture your soul to yourself. However, because of the strong focus that you have upon the physical world, you might find it difficult to create a clear vision of your soul. You can adopt several understandings to help you in your attempt to "see" your soul.

You can begin with the understanding that your soul exists within certain nonphysical realities that are quite different from the familiar physical world. Therefore, your soul can be difficult for you to perceive because its form is different from physical forms. Also, even when you begin to gain a sense of what your soul is like, you will need to remember that your own thoughts and feelings are *creating* the vision of your soul. Thus, it will be important to be honest with yourself as you create the vision of your soul, so that your own confused beliefs do not distort the creation. By noticing any distortions, you can work to eliminate them and thereby refine your vision, bringing it closer to the true reality of your soul.

To begin the creation of your vision of your soul, you can use a simple image to symbolize your soul. Imagine that your soul exists as an invisible cloud of vapor that surrounds and penetrates your body. You cannot see an invisible cloud of vapor, but imagine that this cloud has a certain *vibration of energy*. If it were possible for you to *hear* this vibration, you would experience it as beautiful music. Every time you heard this music, you would realize, "This is my soul."

Now begin to *feel* the energy of your soul. Give yourself to the feeling that arises from the energy form of your soul.

Although your ears cannot hear the energy form of your soul, you have a very delicate inner mechanism through which you can *sense* your soul. This is what was described earlier as your capacity for *spiritual intuition*. This capacity is closely woven with your ability to have feelings—emotions. Ordinarily, this intuitive capacity is overshadowed by the strong emotions and thoughts that you experience in your daily life. However, in this step of your deep attunement process, just as you might hear distant music, you can begin to *feel* your soul through your intuitive capacity.

As you do this step of your deep attunement process, and begin to open to this feeling of your soul, it may at first feel like a certain *unlimitedness*. Or you might have a strong feeling of *purpose* and *meaning*. At times you may experience a deep feeling of *love* and *goodness*. As you become more familiar with these feeling perceptions, you will recognize them as a signal to your conscious mind that tells it to be aware that your soul is within you. Just as when you imagine hearing your soul as music and you say, "Here is my soul," when you feel your soul as these feelings you will say, "Here is my soul." Each time that you experience these special feelings, you will *know* that your soul is present and that it is loving you.

Such feelings are the closest alignment that you can create between your conscious human perceptions and the energies of your soul. Thus, as you set your direction toward an experience of your soul, you can say to yourself:

> **"I begin my search for my soul in my own *feelings*, for that is where I will most clearly recognize the gentle influence of my soul."**

The next phase of setting your direction is to clarify what you will actually be doing during your deep attunement period. You can say it to yourself in this way:

> **"What I am doing in this deep attunement period is adjusting my *conscious awareness* so that I see less of the ordinary physical world, and I see and feel more of the larger spiritual realities. I do not need to *change* myself, nor do I need to *improve* myself to qualify for an experience of my soul. I simply need to change the focus of my human *awareness* so that I can be more aware of the beautiful forces of my soul that are usually hidden behind the opaqueness of ordinary human awareness."**

Remind yourself that in moving toward an experience of your soul, you are making a gentle opening that will invite a subtle, soft experience into your mind and heart. You do not need to strive, push, or force to make this opening. You will take a delicate approach to the opening.

Also, remind yourself again that you do not need to go outside yourself to find your soul. It is present within you each moment. Thus, you do not need to *search for* your soul. You simply need to become consciously aware of it as it presently exists within you.

After you have mastered this, and the previous steps of your attunement process to your satisfaction, add the next step. Always remember to end your attunement period each day with Step Seven, your return to normal awareness.

STEP FIVE:
DEEPENING YOUR EXPERIENCE OF YOUR SOUL

Now that you have set your direction toward an alignment with your soul, the next step to add to your deep attunement process is the deepening of your experience of your soul. Although it was stressed earlier that ideas and concepts are limited, in working with this delicate step it can be helpful to have a concept that can assist you in moving from the ordinary experience of being human to the unusual experience of *consciously* aligning with your soul. If you desire to inwardly "travel" toward a profound experience of your soul, you can use a concept of having a "vehicle" to help you move through "levels of consciousness" in order to gain that larger experience.

You can consider that the vehicle you will use for your ride in the "country of consciousness" is your *awareness*. Just as your automobile can take you from one place in the physical country to another, your awareness can take you from an experience of ordinary reality to an experience of your soul.

To envision this, imagine that you are looking at your toe. Your awareness is focused squarely upon your toe, and for that moment you are aware of nothing else in the universe except your toe. You might call this awareness of your toe a simple, or "low," level of consciousness upon which you have brought your awareness to bear.

Then imagine that you become aware of your whole body. You can say that your awareness has now shifted to a more complex, or "higher," level of consciousness. Your awareness now includes more than it did when you were focused upon your toe.

Next, imagine that you are thinking about yourself and a friend. Your awareness has now shifted to an even more complex, higher level of consciousness.

Then think about your city, next your country, and finally the whole world. In this movement you can say that your *awareness* is taking you through more complex, higher levels of consciousness, one after another. Your awareness is the vehicle that allows your experience to move from one level of consciousness to another.

To extend this concept of awareness, you can ask, "If I am passing through levels of consciousness with my awareness, *what* is being carried along by my awareness? What is riding in the vehicle of awareness?" If you ponder this, you might decide, "That which is being carried along from one level of consciousness to another is me—*myself.*" Thus, to fully understand your movement through various levels of consciousness, from the ordinary human experience to an experience of your soul, it will be important to understand your "Self."

It can be difficult to know clearly what your Self is. You can *feel* your Self quite easily, but to know the full complexity of what you are it is helpful to have something to hold in your mind so that you can think clearly about your Self. For this you can use a simple image of a pool of water. Imagine the pool in stillness. Then imagine the wind stirring the water. Then a leaf falls into the pool. Although different things are happening in the pool, *they are all happening to the same water*.

In the same manner you can consider your Self to be a kind of pool of *energy*, temporarily separated from all other energies in all realities, but still joined to those energies in deep ways of which you are unaware. This temporary pool of energy that is your Self can register many different thoughts, feelings, sensations, ideas, and other experiences, just as the pool of water can be touched in many ways. However, no matter what kind of experience you are having in the pool of energy of your Self, *your Self is always the same*. Your awareness can turn toward many different things, but your *Self* that is experiencing the awareness is always the same energy. The many different things are always happening to the same Self.

Since your Self is always the same, in this moment you are able to feel that you are the same person that you were when you were a child, even though some of your personality patterns of thinking and feeling might have changed. When you are ready for your death, you will feel, "I am the same person that I have always been throughout this lifetime."

This experience of your Self, the sense of "I am me," is *the divine self-awareness* that was projected by you as a soul into your human personality structure before the birth of your present physical body. Thus, you can say that your Self is a dynamic, brilliant *energy construction* created by your soul. *The energy construction of your Self is what is taken by the vehicle of awareness through the various levels of consciousness involved in your movement toward an experience of your soul.*

When your Self changes levels of consciousness it is like the different things happening in the pool of water. What you experience in each level of consciousness will be different, but your Self, which is having the different experiences, remains the same. You will always be you, no matter what level of consciousness you are experiencing. Thus, when your Self goes beyond the ordinary experience of being human, and you begin to have new experiences of your soul, your human Self will still remain the same, for it is your human Self that allows you to remain focused on your life on earth. If you totally released your *human* Self, you would once again become your *eternal* Self—your soul—and you could not remain in a physical body.

As you use this step of your deep attunement process to move toward an experience of your soul, you are simply doing what you have always done throughout your life: *you are being aware of something*. You have done that naturally and easily without needing to work at it. You are always aware of something, some level of consciousness. If you say, "I wish to be aware of *more* than I have been aware of in the past, including a clear experience of my soul," you will be the same Self, but you will be seeking out something *new* to be aware of.

Imagine that you often drive in the country in your automobile, and you always take the same roads and go to the same places. You feel that you do not know how to drive to new places. You do not know where they are. But you can understand that if your automobile is capable of taking you to familiar places, then it certainly has the capacity to take you to new places, as long as you are willing to learn to guide it in new directions. In other words, if your awareness has the capacity to focus on the experiences with which you are familiar, then it has the capacity to focus on new experiences.

This means that in this moment you already have the *abilities* needed to achieve an experience of your soul. You have the capacity to take a journey into new levels of consciousness. Moving to new levels of consciousness involves the very same process of *paying attention* that you use to enter old levels of consciousness. Driving to a new place in your automobile involves the same process of driving that you use to drive to old places. The difference is that since you are not yet familiar with the new levels of consciousness, you do not yet believe that you know how to find them. However, if you can understand that *all roads of consciousness eventually connect to one another*, then you will realize that in order to reach a new place, a new level of consciousness, all that is necessary is *to take the familiar road a bit farther*, and then you will come to the new place.

For example, consider that the human experience of *love* is one of the familiar roads your Self is used to traveling in your vehicle of attention, through the country of consciousness. Thus, you can say that when you are paying attention to the normal experience of love, you are at a familiar level of consciousness. Then you decide that you want to experience your soul. This is a new place in the country of consciousness that you believe you do not know how to find. You can begin the journey by asking yourself, "What do I wish to experience my soul *doing*?" Then you might answer, "I want to experience my soul *loving* me." The experience of normal human love is a familiar road. You have already traveled it in your vehicle of attention. But you have not gone far enough along that road to realize that *the road of normal love eventually leads to a place where your attention can be brought to bear upon the experience of your soul loving you.*

Here is how you can attain an experience of your soul by extending your journey of your Self to larger levels of consciousness during this step of your deep attunement:

Begin by using your imagination to create a level of consciousness of love that is familiar. Create a feeling of love for an important person in your life. Or stir up a feeling of love for yourself. Using your imagination, enter into a feeling of love that you have had in the past. Make that familiar feeling of love as real as possible in this moment. Give yourself easily and naturally to that feeling, without straining or forcing. Let yourself float in that familiar feeling of love.

Now deepen and intensify that feeling of love, and at the same time imagine that same feeling of love *coming into you*. Imagine that love coming from your soul into you.

Then give yourself completely to *both* feelings of love—the feeling of the past normal human love, and the new feeling that you are imagining and creating, which is the feeling of being loved by your soul. Imagine how precious you are to your soul. Imagine the unending love that your soul is pouring into you in this moment. Feel it deeply and fully. Give yourself completely to the feelings.

What begins as an imagination, over a period of time, if you consistently use your creativity and will, can eventually come to be a genuine experience of your soul pouring forth love into your Self. By directing your attention in this manner, you can take yourself from the familiar level of consciousness of loving someone or yourself to the new level of consciousness of experiencing your soul loving you.

It is not important *how* you imagine the movement from one level of consciousness to another. It is important to simply do it. *Any* attempt on your part can trigger an expansion of your awareness that begins the process of moving you toward a new level of consciousness. Again, in this step, you

may even feel that you do not know what you are doing. That does not matter. Simply do anything to initiate the movement that you desire. One experience will lead naturally to another.

This is a *simple* way to guide yourself toward a deeper experience of your soul. If you make the process of experiencing your soul so complicated in your own mind, then you will project before yourself a complicated pathway. You will create a feeling of difficulty, frustration, and expectation of failure. And that will become your experience. You will *create* the complexity by your expectation that the path will be difficult. What you expect is where your awareness will go.

Your Self, with its human awareness, is on the same road as your soul, with its divine awareness. Therefore, to establish an expectation that will lead you where you wish to go, you can say:

> **"I am quite familiar with my Self. Paying attention to my Self is a familiar road. This familiar road leads to my soul. I simply need to go further along this familiar road as I now make my deep attunement, and eventually I will come to my soul."**

In time you will discover that you, as a human being, and you, as an eternal soul, are actually the *same* awareness. You only *appear* to be a separate Self from the human point of view. From your human side of the relationship, you have a small awareness. You are on the "bottom" looking up, but you cannot see the top. As an eternal soul, you are on the top looking down, and you can see all levels.

When you establish within yourself the belief that you and your soul are on the same road, you can use your imagination to project before yourself the expectation of a rather simple journey from your awareness of Self to the experience of your soul. You can create the expectation that you can succeed in that journey. And once you begin to *expect* to succeed, gradually you *will*. You will create your road before you by your expectations and beliefs.

If you believe that the journey to your soul is difficult, then you will begin to expend *effort*. Effort is a road that leads to success and achievement in the *physical* world. The road of effort does not extend directly to your soul. You can consider effort to be a human detour. Even though effort can lead to experiences in the physical world that can be very joyful, you cannot expect to experience the level of consciousness of your soul by straining, forcing, and exerting the kind of effort that achieves success in the physical world.

To reach an experience of your soul, you can move along the road of love, which involves *trust, effortlessness*, and *receptivity*. You will have the kind of experience that you would have sitting in a majestic garden, simply rejoicing in the beauty of the flowers and the peacefulness of the place, not the feeling you would have if you believed that you had to work hard to plant flowers in the garden. You would not strive and strain to *enjoy* the garden. You would simply give yourself to the experience in an effortless, receptive way.

By adopting a belief that your soul is connected to your present Self, and by moving toward your soul by bringing your awareness forward in love, trust, effortlessness, and receptivity, you open a door to the eternal. When you do this consistently in your deep attunement period day after day, you will deepen your experience of your soul.

Each day, after you complete this step, do Step Seven of the attunement process, the return to normal awareness.

STEP SIX: GIVING YOURSELF TO YOUR SOUL

When you are ready to add this step of the deep attunement process, you will be preparing to enter into the most profound experience of your attunement work. However, when you come to this step, you will have done all that you can do with your will. You will have come to the limit of your *human* abilities.

You cannot directly perceive what lies beyond your human experience. Therefore, in order to move farther, you will need to temporarily release your human experience to give in to something unknown that will be brought forward by your soul. You have done your part by walking along the road of love toward your soul. Now it is time for your soul to come forth and meet you, to lead you into the spiritual realms that you cannot directly perceive.

To allow your soul to come forth, you will disengage from everything that you have experienced in the past. You will project yourself beyond the presently known limits of your existence, beyond your present *circle of familiarity*. Anything that you know or have experienced from this lifetime is in your circle of familiarity. As you project yourself beyond that, you give up what you know, what you believe, what you have considered valuable knowledge for your human life. You can begin this release in the following way:

> **Release all that you have created in the previous steps of the deep attunement process, letting those previous experiences slip into the background of your awareness. Allow everything to slip away from your awareness. Let all thoughts and feelings float away. Let your attention drift away from everything. Give up everything that you know and everything that you have experienced. Allow *everything* to gently drift away.**
>
> **In this moment begin to project yourself beyond your circle of familiarity. Let yourself slip comfortably into *not knowing*. Let yourself feel, "I know nothing. I cannot rely upon my mind in this moment. It knows nothing. It is a clean slate. So I do not refer to it now. I now release, and I am free from all that is old. I prepare for newness."**
>
> **In this moment you have no idea what is coming. It is unknown to you, it is unseen. You are calm and poised. You**

**are expectant and trusting. You resist the temptation to try
to guess, or to imagine where your soul will lead you. You
abandon yourself into a delicious expectancy.**

As you succeed in turning your attention away from everything, at first you may perceive nothing except a kind of
inner "blankness." There might be a feeling of emptiness,
which creates the temporary illusion that beyond the physical world there is *nothing*. This "illusion of nothingness"
beyond the physical reality arises because you are normally
so dominated by the intensity of your thoughts and feelings
about the physical world that you are not used to perceiving
the more subtle energies of the spiritual realities. Thus,
when you succeed in turning your attention away from
everything, at first you are not likely to be aware of the spiritual realities. It might take some time to dispel the illusion of
nothingness and allow your soul to guide you to a profound
inner experience of the subtle spiritual energies.

Because of the illusion of nothingness, as you accomplish
this step of the attunement process and allow everything to slip
away, you may believe that you are failing in your attunement
because nothing seems to be happening. You may experience
doubts, and you might even begin to believe that the spiritual
realities do not exist. This is a temporary experience, and it will
pass if you continue to pursue your attunement process with
sensitivity and sincerity.

As you practice this step of your deep attunement process
and come up against the illusion of nothingness—you sit in
the silence and experience only the "blank" inner screen of
your awareness—it is natural to try to use your *will* to attempt
to make something happen. You might try to go somewhere
beyond the blankness, to force yourself to move out of the
experience of nothingness into a spiritual experience.

It is understandable that you would desire to use your will
to *succeed* in having a spiritual experience because you are
used to using your will to succeed in the physical world.

However, if you bring your will forth in an attempt to move beyond the illusion of nothingness, the strong human energies of your will can overpower the delicacy of the moment.

It is very important to realize that if you follow this "natural" impulse to use your will to try to succeed in having a spiritual experience, there are two likely outcomes. First, you can create an inner tension that will tighten your sensitive *intuitive* capacity. This intuitive capacity is needed to penetrate the spiritual realities, which are experienced in a much more subtle and elusive way than your strong, dramatic perceptions of the physical world. The inner tension created by forcing with your will blocks your intuitive opening to spiritual realities, thereby leading your human mind to continue to create an inner blankness in your experience of the attunement moment. This perpetuates the illusion of nothingness.

The second possible result of using your will to try to make something happen is less likely to occur, but it can be much more confusing. In trying to push ahead to success, you can begin to trigger your *imagination*, and you can unknowingly *create* inner visions, or imaginary experiences, that you mistake for actual perceptions of spiritual realities. You would not realize that such visions are an unconscious projection of your human beliefs and ideas about what spiritual realities are supposed to be.

When confronted with the illusion of nothingness in this step of your attunement, the proper use of your will is accomplished in this way:

> **Begin by noticing the impulse within you to try to use your will to make something happen. Then release that impulse without acting upon it. Next, use your will to encourage yourself *to do nothing*. *Accept* the experience of nothingness as the *proper* experience for this moment of your attunement. Know that if you do nothing your soul will now guide you deeper into your attunement experience.**
>
> **This willingness to accept the illusion of nothingness as**

the proper experience opens you to *trust* that if you do nothing to force the moment eventually *the illusion of nothingness will be dissolved for you by your soul*. In time, without any effort on your part, you will find that in this step of your deep attunement, when done steadily and patiently day after day, the illusion of nothingness will begin to dissolve, the human veil of opaqueness will part, and your soul will begin to lead you to a direct experience of the spiritual realities.

The "normal" human use of the will in daily life in the physical world is an *outward, thrusting* movement, as if you are pushing against reality in order to force it to go in the direction that you desire. In this step of your deep attunement, the proper use of the will is an *inward*, taking in, *receiving* movement.

This use of the will—the willingness to give in and to trust that you need do nothing—accomplishes the difficult task of *voluntarily turning your strong human will over to the divine forces of your soul and of God*. By using your will in this manner, you are "giving permission" for the spiritual forces of life to penetrate the normal human veil of opaqueness that ordinarily obscures your perception of spiritual realities.

By being willing to "not do" in the blankness of your attunement, by putting aside your will and trusting that you will be moved along in your attunement process, you release the human stubbornness and stiffness in your personality that is associated with your powerful use of the will in everyday life. You make possible the temporary "overriding" of your limited human capacities by the more powerful abilities of your soul and by the forces of God. In essence, by using your will in this manner, you are temporarily turning your limited personal will over to the unlimited divine will of your soul and of God. This opens the way for the parting of the veil of opaqueness so that you can move toward the perception of the spiritual realities.

Begin now to turn your will over to your soul in the following manner:

Within your experience of this moment, begin to feel something gentle and soft moving closer to you. This is a part of you that is unrecognizable. It is your soul. Since your soul has no form that is perceptible to your human senses, at first there is nothing for you to perceive. Your soul is causing a manifestation that is not perceptible, except as a stirring of a feeling of your soul within you. Begin to feel that hidden within your human personality is an extraordinary being that you are not used to perceiving. Therefore, simply wait expectantly, without exercising old habits of thinking or feeling.

In this moment let yourself feel that your soul is approaching within you in a manner with which you are not familiar. You are willing to resist the temptation to define your soul according to your old mental habits, which are rooted in human reality. In other words, you do not try to give this presence a face, body, personality, or human form of any kind. Instead, you simply feel a loving presence within you, moving closer to your awareness.

In this moment allow your awareness to become a clean slate upon which it now becomes possible to impress a new reality. *As you refuse to try to define this experience in old terms, you give permission for your soul to impress itself upon your awareness in a new way that transcends the limits of your old perceptions.*

Your first clear perception of this impression from your soul can be a feeling of being understood. Feel that a most profound eternal awareness has an absolutely clear knowledge of you as a human being. Feel lovingly understood to the very core of your being.

Accept this without question—without trying to explain it to yourself, without trying to grasp it, without trying to think about it. As long as you refuse to define and precisely delineate, in this moment you can feel your soul embracing

147

you with profound understanding, knowing you with total clarity.

As you accomplish this, you are beginning to assimilate a dimension of your soul that is different from your human life. Do not try to *grasp* this subtle reality, or it will slip away. Inwardly, hold the experience lightly and gently, without stirring, so that the experience can rest softly within you.

As you experiment with this experience day after day, you will actually become merged with the eternal dimensions of your soul. You may not perceive those dimensions in your normal human way, but by gently giving yourself to the experience you gradually *become* that eternal dimension of your soul.

This is a process of being inwardly stimulated that does not use your ordinary human thoughts, which are rooted in physical reality. Accelerate this process in this moment in the following manner:

Continue to open to and invite this experience of your soul. This experience of your soul now comes to you in a way for which you have no symbols. You wish to be very still, without any inward movement. You are having *invisible* experiences. Even though you cannot clearly perceive and understand them, they have a profound impact upon your personality. They begin to create new openings within you. There is an unseen transformation taking place in your personality. By virtue of your desire for a deep experience of your soul, and your willingness to temporarily give up your awareness of old realities, your personality is now being changed in profound ways.

Each day, as you do this step of your deep attunement, you plant a seed of transformation in your personality. As you align with this influence of your soul each day, your thoughts and feelings are affected in ways that will eventually accelerate your *conscious* perceptions. Your awareness will become more illuminated. More and more will your conscious awareness be clearly impressed by the eternal forces of your soul. Gradually, you can learn to consciously perceive the invisible experience of your soul. You can begin to discern a movement, a form, a manifestation that is quite new, which leaves the trace of a new idea, a new kind of thought that you have never before entertained, a new feeling that is larger than what you have felt in the past.

This eventually becomes a merging of your human personality with your soul. Your soul has been waiting for you to desire such a merging with enough intensity that you would be willing to use your human free will to *choose* to make your personality available to a deeper penetration by your soul. Your soul has been waiting for an invitation to enter more deeply into the privacy of your human personality experience. By your willingness to exercise your choice of surrendering yourself, to temporarily release the habitual personality structures that maintain your rigid sense of humanness through thinking, feeling, and identifying with physical objects, you invite a profound experience of your soul.

As you succeed in using your will in this way, you turn yourself over to your soul. In time you will feel the loving presence of your soul quite consistently. You will feel the love of your soul drawing you into deep experiences that will be your soul's gift to you, the human personality. These experiences cannot be imagined or anticipated. They cannot be described. They will have a quality that will be precisely what you need to experience in the moment in which you are existing. Your soul will lead you in ways that you cannot conceptualize. You can only release and trust, and allow your soul to guide you.

This profound stage of your deep attunement is a very personal, unique communication between your human Self and your soul. All that you need do is prepare the way for this moment by accomplishing each step of the attunement process up to this point as honestly and lovingly as you can. After that, you will simply release. Do it in this way:

> Release yourself into the love and wisdom of your soul,
> and rejoice in the experience. Let your soul take you where
> you need to go. Enter into the magnificence of all dimen-
> sions of life, guided by your soul, and allow your human Self
> to celebrate the goodness and love of all of life.

Continue this final step of your deep attunement process for
as long as you desire. Then, when you feel that the experience of that attunement period is complete, it will be time to
do Step Seven and return to your human existence in the
physical world.

STEP SEVEN: RETURNING TO YOUR HUMAN LIFE

Over time, as you deepen your attunement experience, you
will find that during the above step of your attunement
process you can "wander" far from your normal human
awareness. Therefore, after each attunement period, when
you decide that it is time to return to your normal state of
consciousness, it will be very important to take your time
and bring yourself back *slowly*.

To return to your normal awareness, you will use the
same ability to shift your awareness that you did in moving
toward your soul. You will be returning back along the same
pathway that you previously traveled. This can be accomplished in the following manner:

> In this moment begin to let go of the expanded awareness
> that you have created during your attunement period. Let
> there come a feeling of gentle movement back toward your
> strong feeling of yourself. Do this slowly, taking as much
> time as you need to let go of the expanded awareness that
> you have attained.
>
> As you do this, remind yourself that you are returning to
> your human life with a renewed conviction that you are

deeply loved by your soul. Remind yourself that throughout your day, in each moment you are loved by your soul.

As you continue to slowly and gradually release your expanded awareness, begin to turn your attention to your physical body. Notice sensations that you might feel in various parts of your body. You may even begin to slowly and gently move various parts of your body, such as your hands or feet. Continue to notice your body until you feel that you are solidly existing in a normal way inside your physical body.

Begin now to turn your attention to your outer physical surroundings. With your eyes still closed, begin to notice what you are hearing around you. Begin to think about where you are. Feel yourself sitting solidly where you are. Feel yourself comfortably contained in your physical surroundings.

Next, begin to think about what you will do when your attunement period is over. Let your mind drift toward your daily affairs and briefly look them over.

Then tell yourself that you are becoming very alert. You are feeling refreshed and rejuvenated. You are eager to reenter your daily life with the love and inspiration that you have gained from your attunement period.

When you feel completely ready, gently open your eyes. Sit for a moment or two so that you can regain your equilibrium, then slowly rise and joyfully resume your activities in the physical world.

YOUR SPIRITUAL PATHWAY

As you work with this deep attunement process, you can gain such an inspiring experience of your soul that you might decide that you wish to walk a spiritual pathway every day of your life. The key to a successful spiritual pathway is your willingness to bring your spiritual experiences from your deep attunement periods to your *ordinary* human affairs each day.

A spiritual pathway is simply your personal dedication to constantly remain open to the spiritual realities that sustain human life. It is your willingness to consistently try to experience more than appears on the surface of physical life. It is your daily work to expand your awareness to include the forces of your soul and of God in everything that you do in the physical world. It is your ongoing commitment to continually strive to bring together the human and the divine in every moment of your life.

Your spiritual path begins in your human experience, with the simple day-to-day willingness to be honest, kind, and loving to the best of your ability. At other times it involves working courageously and honestly with feelings of fear or pain that may arise in your human experience. If you do not strengthen your human abilities to experience all of life in a creative way, you might find that you can only feel your soul and God during your attunement period, or during special holy moments of prayer. However, if you open your full human abilities of thought, emotion, and intuition, you can eventually experience your soul and God *everywhere in life*.

To guide yourself along your spiritual pathway, you can say to yourself each day:

> **"I begin my spiritual pathway by my willingness to be human, to live my human life honestly, courageously, and lovingly. Each day I will look for the beauty of my soul and of God in myself, in other people, and in all of life. *If I can find the magnificence of my soul and of God in my moment-to-moment human experience, then I can find it everywhere.*"**

As you live your daily life in this way, then when you use the deep attunement process each day to align with your soul, you will find that your attunement experience will be richer, more joyful, and more beautiful. You will be able to bring that richness back into your daily affairs, manifesting the beauty of your soul more fully in your expression in the physical world.

CHAPTER SEVEN

Your Transformation

———— ✳ ————

N ow that you have learned how to draw upon the forces of your soul, as you continue to practice your attunement each day you can look forward to many exhilarating changes in your life.

One of the first changes is likely to be an awakening to your *full potential* as a human being. Your attunement to your soul can free you from past limits of negative thinking, feeling, and choosing, enabling you to attain a clearer vision of your true potential. In your limited experiences in the past, it was as though you had gone to a brilliant play and fallen asleep in the middle. Then when you awoke at the end you said, "It was not a good play," forgetting that you had slept through most of it.

In awakening to the full potential within your human personality, it is as though you are returning to the play, but now you are staying awake through the entire performance. In other words, in your limited experiences in the past, you did not see all of your talents, abilities, and positive qualities—you fell asleep in the middle of your play—and you created a feeling that said, "I am not good enough." After your awakening, you will see the true brilliance of the vast, limitless potential within you, and you will begin to draw more fully upon that potential each day. Using more of your potential will lead to feelings of greater self-confidence and strength. You will begin to act more powerfully in your day-to-day life, and you will experience a deep sense of joy and fulfillment as you express yourself with greater and greater freedom.

As you continue to deepen your attunement process, not only will you see all of your play in the theater of human expression, but you will also go backstage and meet the actors in the play. In other words, you will begin to see *beneath* the surface of your human experience to your underlying motives and purposes. You will see behind the scenes of your human thoughts, feelings, and choices. In time you can discover previously hidden patterns from this lifetime, and from your past human lifetimes, that have been influencing the way you are living.

Another change that you can bring about through your attunement is a deepening of your experience of love. You will feel a deeper love for yourself and a greater desire to love other people. You will be inspired to use your unfolding power to give more to others, bringing about more satisfying relationships in all areas, from friendships to deep, intimate relationships.

You can also expect a stronger expression of your *intuitive* abilities. By learning to use your intuition to feel your soul in greater depth, you will stimulate your ability to use your intuition in daily life. You might begin to feel that you are knowing other people in a deeper, intuitive way. You might intuitively sense important underlying connections between yourself and others. It is possible that your intuition will extend to sensing events that will happen in the future, or to an opening of psychic abilities that you may have.

As you open your intuition more and more, you will most likely notice a growing richness in your dreams. They should become clearer and easier to understand. As a result, the guidance that you receive from your soul during the sleep state will be able to reach your conscious awareness with less distortion from your personality patterns. In time, as you continue your growth, your dreams can become a valuable source of wisdom and inspiration.

You can also become more sensitive to the guidance that is given to you by your soul and by other souls during your waking hours. The sense of being prompted in positive, creative ways can become stronger as you practice using your intuitive abilities. Bringing together your human intelligence and experience in the physical world with a deep sensing of true inner guidance will enable you to make life choices with much more confidence and success.

From the consistent practice of your attunement, you can also expect to release a powerful creativity into everything that you do. You will be able to infuse your work and play activities with potent new ideas and creative impulses. If you choose to express your creativity in artistic ways, such as painting, writing, and music, you can expect a dramatic new flowering of creative impulses that will greatly expand your artistic expression.

Another change that you can expect is a greater sensitivity to the majesty of life. Not only will you become acutely aware and appreciative of the beauty of nature, but you will also begin to have an experience of a larger magnificence in life that is not limited to the confines of physical reality. You will feel a most incredible beauty that extends beyond the horizons of birth and death. You will experience the extraordinary splendor of the spiritual dimensions of life.

FUTURE TRANSFORMATIONS

As all of these fulfilling and stimulating changes take place in your life, there will come a moment in which you will realize: "I am being completely *transformed* by the powerful experiences that I am creating through my attunement process and day-to-day growth." Your inner work will bring about a transformation in every area of your life, setting the stage for illuminating new experiences in the future that will go beyond anything that you have imagined in this lifetime.

Your expanded experiences will lead you to *future transformations* that will take place in four areas. To understand those transformations, it can be helpful to have a clear vision of them to carry with you in your day-to-day life. Just as you were given four pillars to inspire your personal growth, in order to establish a vision that does justice to the scope and scale of your future transformations, you can build that vision upon four ideals that can be your four *pillars of transformation*.

Some of the transformations that will now be described will take place in your present lifetime. Others may be expressed in future lifetimes. Although you might feel that some of the transformations are beyond your present ability to attain in this lifetime, it is important to release any feelings of limit about what you can accomplish, and to realize that what is described in the four visions of transformation is what your soul *intends* for you to experience. The four visions describe what you *will* eventually attain. The amount of time it will take will be determined by *the degree of your commitment to unfolding the many aspects of your human personality expression in honesty and love.*

THE FIRST PILLAR OF TRANSFORMATION:
YOUR FUTURE EXPERIENCE OF YOUR HUMAN SELF

As you continue your transformation in this lifetime, you will become more aware of the thoughts and feelings that squeeze the truth out of your life. You will learn how to recognize the patterns of thinking, feeling, and choosing that you create that cause you to temporarily lose sight of the eternal harmony and beauty. And you will heal those patterns with wisdom and love.

From that healing, your transformation will expand. You will be able to more fully align your daily thoughts and feelings with kindness, compassion, honesty, idealism, and love. Then your thoughts and feelings will take on a different quality. They will actually be changed in their *energy structures*. The energies of those new thoughts and feelings will become more creatively powerful and potent, and they will begin to *amplify* and *magnify* the eternal forces that are flowing into earth life.

As you continue transforming the energies of your thoughts and feelings, your experience of your human *Self* will be changed in remarkable ways. The change can be seen clearly through a comparison between the present and the future.

Usually, in your *present* experience you feel some joy and goodness *when all goes well in your daily affairs*. The rest of the time you can feel the pressure of your earth challenges—the busyness, the complexity, some fear here, some doubt and worry there. Occasionally, you might feel some despair. Perhaps at times you even feel a great dread. Because of these negative experiences in the outer world, you can often feel, "Life is not good." This subjective experience that you are *creating* blocks your vision of the truth that the underlying nature of life is *always* wonderful, whether your *experience* of life pleases you or not.

After your transformation in your experience of your Self, you will awaken each morning and instantly feel a thrill of excitement about, and a deep gratitude for, the opportunity to live in a physical body, and to think and feel as one individual human being. No matter *what* you are thinking or feeling, whether it happens to be pleasant or unpleasant, you will feel the vast connections of important purposes and meanings within the experience.

You will not be like a child who must be constantly pleased in order to be happy. You will be a powerful virtuoso of human experience who can relish every moment of life, even moments that bring change and complexity. No matter what experience each moment might hold, you will feel the passion and excitement of being alive in your human form in that moment, *knowing that you are accomplishing purposes that are important in the unfoldment of your personal expression through many human lifetimes.*

You will go forth each day with a fulfilling sense of intense aliveness and personal creativity. You will consistently feel a great joy and a deep love. You will feel a strong sense of wholeness, even in a kaleidoscopic changing expression each day. In the future, because of the exceptional unfoldment of the human intellect, and the diversifying of subtleties of human emotion that will occur, human life will become more and more complex. However, your personal experience of that complexity will be powerfully positive and creative.

Habits of despair and depression will be gone, mastered, healed. You will have a strong and clear understanding of all your human motives, the reasons underlying your daily choices, and the deep purpose and meaning of all your thoughts and feelings. You will attain an exceptional knowledge of your human psychology and a remarkable authority over the human personality expression.

You will then become not a slave to the human personality patterns of thinking and feeling, but a *master* of that personality. You will *choose* and *direct*, in a loving, creative manner, the way that you think, feel, and act in the world.

THE SECOND PILLAR OF TRANSFORMATION:
YOUR FUTURE EXPERIENCE OF LOVED ONES

Imagine that you are a primitive human being in prehistoric times. You are concerned only with your own pleasures— eating, sleeping, sexual fulfillment, and so forth. All that matters to you is what satisfies your personal desires. You have no interest in other human beings except as objects for your own pleasure.

This can be seen as an exaggerated example of the *least* creative way to have relationships with other human beings, a simplified symbol of the selfishness that maintains the experience of *separation* from other human beings. This is part of a past expression from which human beings are emerging.

As you carry out your personal transformation, you build toward a future in which you will move to the *positive* extreme in human relationships. You will clearly realize that you are not an isolated Self. You will understand that the past experience of isolation was simply a temporary illusion that enabled you to have a more *intense* human experience. As you become more and more enlightened, the illusion of separation will be shattered.

As the illusion of separation from others is dissolved, you will still feel the wonderful sense of your own Self—your own unique existence as an individual human being—and you will continue to perceive your loved ones as discreet individuals, but you will see and feel the strong energies of love that are constantly flowing between yourself and them. Those energies of love will come into your awareness naturally, as part of your normal perception of reality. You will know without doubt that those bonds of love between yourself and your loved ones are more real and important than your temporary human physical bodies.

With each individual loved one in your life, you will feel much more than a love that depends upon them satisfying you and bringing you pleasure. You will feel a love that cuts to the very core of your being, so that you will care as much for every one of them, for their lives and well-being, as you do for your own. You will experience a profound *merging* of your personality with theirs. Although you will continue to have a discreet sense of personal Self, there will be a marvelous feeling of *belonging together* that is based upon *an enlightened awareness of new bonds of love that you are continually weaving with the loved ones in your life*.

This does not mean that there will be an absence of differences and unique personal qualities. It means that you will be able to enter into the different personal expressions of your loved ones with a joyful feeling that their particular qualities belong to you because they themselves are part of you.

All of the personal love relationships that you choose to establish and commit to, whether they are family relationships, deep friendships, or intimate, romantic relationships, will reach the extraordinary level of fulfillment that you have always desired. You will finally satisfy the hunger for personal love that has driven you through many lifetimes.

THE THIRD PILLAR OF TRANSFORMATION:
YOUR FUTURE AWARENESS OF SPIRITUAL REALITIES

As you unfold your full human potential by loving and growing, you carry forth long-standing patterns that you have been refining through many past lifetimes. You can imagine this complex unfoldment of your overall human expression through many lifetimes as the nurturing of a beautiful rosebush. There are many seasons in the life of this plant. At times the flowers are blooming and beautiful. At other times the rosebush is resting and renewing itself, and there are no flowers. There are different stages of growth.

If you *nurture* the rosebush, the growth is beautiful. The blossoms are wonderful. *The full potential of the plant is expressed through all of its seasons*.

In terms of your experience of spiritual realities, this means that in each lifetime if you make the *nurturing, growthful, loving* choices in your human experience, then your ability to experience spiritual realities will fully blossom. The rosebush of your human spiritual expression will grow magnificently through all of its seasons. There will be wonder and beauty in your experience of your soul, and in your awareness of the spiritual realms.

In this lifetime, as you bring about your transformation through a dedication to healing, truth, idealism, and love, you are nurturing your rosebush of human expression through its *present* season, and you are moving toward a future in which the blossoms will become even more beautiful. You are creating a strong momentum that will eventually enable you to sit in the silence of your attunement, release the distractions of the physical world, and then *immediately perceive your own soul standing before you in a form that is wonderful and majestic.* You will quite clearly understand: "This soul is *me.* And in this moment *I feel myself existing in my soul form and my human form at the same time.*" This experience will bring the most astounding sense of joy and transcendence.

As you deepen your attunement even more, your spiritual experience will expand beyond the awareness of your own soul. Eventually, in the silence of your attunement, you will see standing before you *many* souls who are joined to you in love. In very intense ways you will feel yourself to be a part of them, and a part of their vast creation of human life on earth.

Then, as you continue your commitment to truth, in time, while you are in human form, it will be possible for you to clearly perceive and *experience* what human beings have considered throughout the ages to be *God.* Such perceptions and experiences are so vast, so different from present human experience, that there are no words for them. You will experience those realities in ways that transcend all words and thoughts.

THE FOURTH PILLAR OF TRANSFORMATION:
YOUR FUTURE EXPERIENCE OF HUMANITY

In your future enlightenment that will come from your steady commitment to healing, love, and truth, *your relationship to humanity will be one of the most powerful and important accomplishments that you will make in your human existence.* It will become the "capstone" of the monument of your human expression.

As you exist in your present moment, you naturally feel, "I am *here* with the people with whom I have a personal relationship, and *there* is the rest of humanity." Those close to you are more important than other people. You have a deeper relationship with them. All others are strangers, and strangers are less significant to you.

In the future you will realize that *there are no strangers*. Your vision will become so powerful that you will see through not only the illusion of separation between yourself and those human beings that you know personally, but also through the appearance of separation from strangers. You will literally see all about the earth *the instreaming, connecting energies from the eternal souls of every living human being*. You will *feel* those connections as though they are a celestial orchestra of life. You will feel the power and the extraordinary beauty of those forces as they weave all beings into the cosmic fabric of what you would consider to be God. Then you will understand that the forces of God have many manifestations in many realms, but in the *physical* realm the most magnificent manifestation is *the expression of the entire human race on earth, from the beginning of time and space to the end of that phase of manifestation*.

CHARTING YOUR FUTURE COURSE

Each day, in the choices that you make, you are deciding the direction of the rest of your life. What you choose will set the course not only for this lifetime but for future expressions that you will have as a human being on earth as well.

To chart your course wisely it is beneficial to work each day to expand your *beliefs* about life. Such an expansion will enable you to continually heal narrow beliefs that can hide the truth from you. For example, imagine that you are a spiritual pilgrim in search of the truth. You are wandering in a forest and you come upon a circle of men. Their clothing is dirty, their hair and beards unkempt. When you see them, you say, "Here is a group of vagabonds. They are probably cruel, unkind, and devious. I will pass them by." Then later you discover that they were wise men who knew the truth that you so desperately desired. You were blinded by your mistaken *belief* about who they were.

As you set your course for the future, you can encourage yourself to expand your beliefs toward a clearer reflection of truth by saying to yourself each day:

> **"As long as I am in human form, what I experience each day will be determined by my *beliefs* about life. If I am willing to expand my beliefs until I can believe *there is an underlying goodness in all of life*, whether I can feel that goodness or not, then my beliefs will enable me to *direct* my subjective experience toward the truth."**

If you do not choose to *direct* your experience toward the truth of life—toward harmony, growth, honesty, compassion, idealism, and love—then such experiences will be difficult to bring about on a consistent basis. Because of the inherent selfish tendency of the "animal" nature that you have taken on as part of your human personality expression in a physical body, if your personality is simply left alone in self-involvement and you do nothing to *choose* goodness, you will tend to drift away from truth.

This means that your largest responsibility to yourself is *to choose truth, and to commit to it, day by day throughout your life.* Then your subjective experience of life—your thoughts, feelings, and beliefs—will begin to blossom fully. They will become more joyful, beautiful, and satisfying. They will more clearly reflect the underlying magnificence of reality through all of its phases, human and divine.

Throughout this book the tremendous *power* that you hold in your hand—the power of your *choice*—has been stressed. You exercise that power with each *thought*, *feeling*, and *action* that you choose. If you choose to live each day focused upon selfishness and negativity, then you are using that power to create darkness, pain, and suffering for this lifetime. Such a creation is not a reflection of the true nature of life. It is a temporary human distortion.

If you choose to live each day to the best of your ability, committing yourself to *honesty, kindness, compassion, love*, and *idealism*, then through your *choice* you are using the creative power of God itself to not only create goodness in your personal experience of life but to also bring that power into tangible manifestation in the physical world. Your manifestation then becomes part of the uplifting transformation that is beginning to unfold on earth.

To inspire yourself to chart a future course that leads to transformation and truth, you can remind yourself each day:

> **"With my freedom to choose what to think and feel, and how to act in the world,** *I hold the power of life itself in my hand.* **Each day I must** *decide* **how to use that power.** *What I decide becomes my contribution to human existence on earth. It also determines the course that I will follow in this lifetime and in future lifetimes."*

When you chart your course in alignment with truth, you will gain an unshakable certainty that you are a creative and dynamic eternal soul expressing yourself through many human lifetimes in the physical world. You will know that your true purpose in those many lifetimes is *to experience a full completion of your human existence while manifesting the magnificence of your eternal soul and the forces of God into the physical world.* Following your course toward truth, you will go forth to the accomplishment of that purpose day by day, throughout this lifetime.

Appendix A

OUTLINE OF ATTUNEMENT METHOD
FOR CHAPTER FIVE,
"YOUR BEGINNING ATTUNEMENT"

The following outline of the beginning attunement method presented in Chapter Five, "Your Beginning Attunement," can serve as a quick reference guide. Once you have thoroughly digested the description of each step of the technique as presented in Chapter Five, and you are familiar with doing the attunement, you can refer to this simplified outline to guide yourself through the steps of the beginning attunement process.

Only excerpts from the instructions in Chapter Five are presented here. As you use this outline, if you forget any of the explanations, refer back to Chapter Five.

STEP ONE: RETREATING FROM THE WORLD

Seek out a place of beauty and peacefulness where you will have complete privacy for your entire attunement period.

STEP TWO: RELAXING YOUR BODY

Sit comfortably with your body in a position that you can hold without any strain. Experiment until you find the most comfortable position.

After you are comfortable, close your eyes. Take a few deep breaths. Then begin to relax your body. Silently speak relaxing words to yourself. Your body will follow your silent command to release tension. Say to yourself inwardly: "In this moment I let go of all tension in my body. My body is now relaxing. It is becoming very loose and flexible. All effort is now being released. My body is relaxing deeply now. It is entering such a deep, calm state of relaxation that I feel wonderfully restful and content." Do this for as long as you desire.

Next, turn your attention, in a slow, gentle way, to your breathing. Simply notice your breathing, not trying to do anything special with it. Gently become aware of your breathing, and continue to relax.

STEP THREE:
RELEASING YOUR THOUGHTS AND EMOTIONS

As you sit in the silence, in a calm, patient way allow your ordinary thoughts and emotions to simply drift away, instead of trying to eliminate them. Let your attention wander into an "area above" your thoughts and emotions, as though your attention is gently and effortlessly floating away. You can feel that your thoughts and emotions are heavy energies that are sinking down and slipping out of your awareness, while your awareness is a joyful inner field of focus that is light and airy, slowly and softly lifting up. You are riding that light, airy awareness as it gradually floats upward, away from your heavier thoughts and emotions.

STEP FOUR:
PROJECTING BEYOND THE HUMAN

Begin to imagine yourself floating upward, out of your ordinary experience. You are leaving behind the physical earth and your ordinary human perceptions. Imagine that you are now turning toward a new experience of freedom. Imagine that you are preparing to move toward your soul.

Next, begin to imagine that you are a nonphysical being floating freely above the physical earth. You are floating in a marvelous existence of *love*.

STEP FIVE: GAINING INTENSITY AND DEPTH

Begin to imagine that as you float in a beautiful realm of love, you are now *becoming the love*. Use your will to give yourself to a free-floating experience in which, even though you may not know exactly how to imagine becoming love, you do it nonetheless. Using your will, set your intention to become the love that you have imagined.

After you set your intention, release. Simply become the feeling of love.

STEP SIX: RELEASING INTO YOUR SOUL

Begin to give up all willing and striving. Give up all desire to *do*. Release yourself into simply *being*. Become the experience of the moment, without exerting any personal influence over the moment or trying to control it. Become softness and *receptivity*, without striving. Simply release yourself into a gentle current that will carry you toward your soul. Release completely and allow your soul to carry you toward the experience you need in the moment.

STEP SEVEN: RETURNING TO NORMAL AWARENESS

Begin to slowly let go of the expanded awareness that you attained during your attunement period. Let the experience of expansion begin to drift away. Create a feeling of gently moving back toward your ordinary experience of yourself. Do this quite slowly, taking as much time as you need to return to your normal awareness.

Next, turn your attention to your physical body. Notice how your body feels. Pay attention to any physical sensations that you are experiencing.

Then begin to pay attention to the room about you. Notice what the air feels like. Listen for sounds in the outer world.

Next, begin to think about your daily affairs and what you will do in the physical world. Create a feeling of eagerness to take up the activities of your daily life with a new sense of inspiration and rejuvenation.

When you feel completely ready, slowly open your eyes. Sit for a moment or two so that you can regain your equilibrium, then slowly rise and joyfully resume your activities in the physical world.

Appendix B

OUTLINE OF ATTUNEMENT METHOD
FOR CHAPTER SIX,
"A DEEPER EXPERIENCE OF YOUR SOUL"

———— ✳ ————

The following outline of the deep attunement method presented in Chapter Six, "A Deeper Experience of Your Soul," can serve as a quick reference guide. Once you have digested the description of each step of the technique as presented in Chapter Six, and you are familiar with doing the attunement, you can refer to this outline to guide yourself through the steps of the deep attunement process.

Only excerpts from the instructions in Chapter Six are presented here. As you use this outline, if you forget any of the explanations, refer back to Chapter Six.

STEP ONE:
BEGINNING YOUR DEEP ATTUNEMENT

Sit comfortably with your eyes closed. Take a few deep breaths. Continue to relax your body. Silently speak relaxing words to yourself. Say to yourself inwardly: "In this moment I release all tension in my thoughts, emotions, and body. My body is now relaxing more and more. I am now entering a deep, calm state of relaxation. I feel completely relaxed and very peaceful."

Next, notice your breathing. Without any effort, simply

become aware of it. Do not try to adjust your breathing or control it. Simply notice it, and continue to relax.

STEP TWO:
RELEASING PHYSICAL REALITY

Direct your inner awareness away from your thoughts. Use your inner sensing to feel beyond your thoughts. Allow your thoughts to drift away. Let your attention wander beyond your thoughts. Let your attention gently float away from your thoughts. Allow your awareness to drift gently upward, above your thoughts.

Then imagine that you are beginning to drift away from the physical world. You are beginning to slowly float upward above the earth. You are feeling yourself leaving behind all heaviness, all burdens. You are floating away from all physical reality.

STEP THREE:
CREATING HARMONY AND LOVE

Accepting and ignoring any thoughts that might arise, gently use your will to pay attention to your imagination. Direct your imagination to align with your intuitive capacity in order to begin the creation of your inner landscape of harmony and love. Initiate this by imagining a *setting* that inspires feelings of harmony and love in you.

As you begin this imagining, invite feelings of harmony and love into your heart. Also imagine that the powerful intuitive capacity that lives within you is coming forward into the moment. Inwardly feel that you are intuitively aligning with a deep inner wisdom within you.

Next, use your imagination to place yourself fully into the inner landscape that you have created. Enter that landscape and begin to live within it with great abandonment and joy.

Next, turn your attention to the force that unites all

beings in all realms of existence—the force of *love*. Be aware that a divine *energy* of love permeates all of life, and there is also the human *feeling* of love. Use your imagination and creativity to try to bring them both together in the beautiful inner landscape that you have created.

Next, in your inner landscape, as you attune to this love, begin to imagine that you are surrounded by loving souls who share the wonder of existence with you. Feel surrounded by beloved ones of an exalted nature. Feel joined to them by the energy of the love.

STEP FOUR:
SETTING YOUR DIRECTION

Imagine your soul surrounding you with love. Begin to feel the energy of your soul. Give yourself to the feeling that arises from its energy. Open your spiritual intuition through which you can sense your soul. Feel your soul through your intuition.

Be aware that your soul is within you. *Know* that your soul is present and that it is loving you.

STEP FIVE:
DEEPENING YOUR EXPERIENCE OF YOUR SOUL

Create a feeling of love for an important person in your life or stir up a feeling of love for yourself. Using your imagination, enter into the feeling of love. Make that feeling as real as possible in this moment. Give yourself easily and naturally to that feeling, without straining or forcing. Let yourself float in that familiar feeling of love.

Now deepen and intensify that feeling of love, and at the same time imagine that same feeling of love *coming into you*. Imagine that love coming from your soul into you.

Then give yourself completely to *both* feelings of love— the feeling of the past normal human love, and the new feeling that you are imagining and creating, which is the feeling of being loved by your soul. Imagine how precious you are to your soul. Imagine the unending love that your soul is pouring into you in this moment. Feel it deeply and fully. Give yourself completely to the feelings.

STEP SIX: GIVING YOURSELF TO YOUR SOUL

Release all that you have created in the previous steps of the deep attunement process, letting those previous experiences slip into the background of your awareness. Allow everything to slip away from your awareness. Let all thoughts and feelings float away. Let your attention drift away from everything. Give up everything that you know, and everything that you have experienced. Allow *everything* to gently drift away.

In this moment begin to project yourself beyond your circle of familiarity. Let yourself slip comfortably into *not knowing*. Let yourself feel, "I know nothing. I cannot rely upon my mind in this moment. It knows nothing. It is a clean slate. So I do not refer to it now. I now release, and I am free from all that is old. I prepare for newness."

In this moment you have no idea what is coming. It is unknown to you, it is unseen. You are calm and poised. You are expectant and trusting. You resist the temptation to try to guess, or to imagine where your soul will lead you. You abandon yourself into a delicious expectancy. Know that if you do nothing your soul will now guide you deeper into your attunement experience.

Within your experience of this moment, begin to feel something gentle and soft moving closer to you. This is your soul. In this moment let yourself feel that your soul is approaching within you. Feel a loving presence within you, moving closer to your awareness.

Allow your soul to impress itself upon your awareness in a new way that transcends the limits of your old perceptions.

Feel that your soul has an absolutely clear knowledge of you as a human being. Feel lovingly understood to the very core of your being. Feel your soul embracing you with profound understanding, knowing you with total clarity.

Release yourself into the love and wisdom of your soul, and rejoice in the experience. Let your soul take you where you need to go. Enter into the magnificence of all dimensions of life, guided by your soul, and allow your human Self to celebrate the goodness and love of all life.

STEP SEVEN: RETURNING TO YOUR HUMAN LIFE

In this moment begin to let go of the expanded awareness that you have created during your attunement period. Let there come a feeling of gentle movement back toward your strong feeling of yourself. Do this slowly, taking as much time as you need to let go of the expanded awareness that you have attained.

As you continue to slowly and gradually release your expanded awareness, begin to turn your attention to your physical body. Notice sensations that you might feel in various parts of your body. You may even begin to slowly and gently move various parts of your body, such as your hands or feet. Continue to notice your body until you feel that you are solidly existing in a normal way inside your physical body.

Begin now to turn your attention to your outer physical surroundings. With your eyes still closed, begin to notice what you are hearing around you. Begin to think about where you are. Feel yourself sitting solidly where you are. Feel yourself comfortably contained in your physical surroundings.

Next, begin to think about what you will do when your attunement period is over. Let your mind drift toward your daily affairs and briefly look over them.

Then tell yourself that you are becoming very alert. You

are feeling refreshed and rejuvenated. You are eager to reenter your daily life with the love and inspiration that you have gained from your attunement period.

When you feel completely ready, slowly open your eyes. Sit for a moment or two so that you can regain your equilibrium, then slowly rise and joyfully resume your activities in the physical world.

For more information about Dr. Scolastico's work, write to:
Transpersonal Consultation Group
Post Office Box 6556
Woodland Hills, CA 91365